IPHONE 15

USER GUIDE

The Complete Step By Step Instruction Manual With Illustrations To Help Beginners And Seniors Master The New iPhone 15 Plus. With Tips & Tricks For iOS

By

Donald L. McGuire

Table of Contents

Chapter One

The iPhone Plus

Find out where everything on the iPhone 15 Plus, such as the cameras, buttons, and ports, is located.

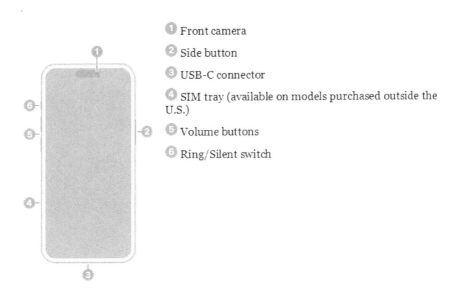

1. Front camera
2. Side button
3. USB-C connector
4. SIM tray (available on models purchased outside the U.S.)
5. Volume buttons
6. Ring/Silent switch

The new iPhone 15 Plus from the front. The front-facing camera is located in the upper middle. The side button is on the right side. The Lightning port is located at the underside. The SIM card slot, the volume controls, and the ringer/mute toggle may all be found on the left side of the device.

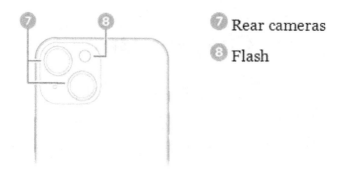

⑦ Rear cameras

⑧ Flash

iPhone 15 Plus, seen from the rear. The camera and flash for the back are located on the upper left.

Activate Siri On Your iPhone

Use just your voice to do common chores. Use Siri
to have a word translated, an alarm set, directions, a
weather report, and more.

Siri responds to a request for an alarm at 8:00 AM.

Indicates that Siri is listening.

A display on an iPhone. An alert from the Clock app indicates that an alarm has been set for 8:00 a.m. and appears at the screen's top. An indicator at the bottom of the screen shows that Siri is listening.

Install Siri

The following are options for activating Siri if you skipped that step while setting up your iPhone:

- To voice activate Siri: Go to Settings > Siri & Search, hit "Listen for," then pick "Hey Siri" or "Siri" (if you have that choice).
  For compatible iPhones, the option to use the name "Siri" alone is available in various languages and countries.
- To trigger Siri with a push of a button: Select Siri & Search from the main menu, then toggle Press Side Button for Siri (on a Face ID-enabled iPhone) or Press Home for Siri (on a device without Face ID).

Use your voice to activate Siri
When activated by speech, Siri provides an audible response.

Just call out "Siri" or "Hey, Siri," and then your query or request will be heard.

Try asking, "Hey Siri, what's the weather like today?" or "Siri, wake me up at 8 o'clock"

Put your iPhone face down or go to Settings > Siri & Search > touch "Listen for," and then choose Off to disable the iPhone's ability to react to the phrases "Hey Siri" or "Siri."

When using an AirPods device that is compatible with Siri, you may activate Siri by just speaking.

Push-button Siri activation

When the iPhone is set to quiet mode, Siri still answers when activated by a button. Siri's responses are audible when the quiet mode is disabled.

1. Pick one of these options:
   - Hold the side button on an iPhone equipped with Face ID.
   - If your iPhone has a physical Home button, press and hold it.
   - To make a call using your EarPods, press and hold the center button.
   - To use CarPlay, either press and hold the steering wheel button designated for voice commands or tap and hold the Home button when in CarPlay's main interface.
   - To use Siri Hands-Free while driving, press and hold the voice command button.
2. Make a request or ask a question.

   Put it like this: "What is 18 percent of 225?" or "Set the timer for 3 minutes."

On AirPods that support it, you can also activate Siri by touching them together.

Inquire in quick succession

You don't have to reactivate Siri if you have more questions after you've asked it anything.

1. Invoke Siri and then issue your demand.
2. Immediately after you make the request, make another one.

Interrupt Siri while it's talking to cancel a request.

Say something like, "Hey Siri, what's the weather like in San Francisco today?" Where does Cupertino fit in?

If Siri gets anything wrong, you can fix it

Use a new wording for your request.

- Tap the Listen button, and then rephrase your request if you aren't making consecutive requests.
- Provide some specifics about what you want: If Siri doesn't comprehend a word you say, tap the Listen button and spell it out again. Use the person's full name after saying "Call," for instance.
- Modifies a message just before it is sent Replace the phrase with "Change it."
- If your request appears on the screen, you may make changes to it by typing in new content. To respond, tap the request and type using the on-screen keyboard.

- Make the new, improved request right after the old one to avoid having to reactivate Siri. (In certain locations and countries, this feature is compatible with specific iPhone models.)

Instead of talking to Siri, just type

1. You may activate Type to Siri by going to Settings > Accessibility > Siri.
2. Siri must be activated before a user may put a request into the text box and keyboard.

Enlarge The iPhone Display

Many applications allow you to magnify or reduce the size of an image. You may double-tap or squeeze to see more detail in Photos, and you can enlarge the width of the columns on a site in Safari. No matter what you're doing, the Zoom function will allow you to see every detail on the screen. You may either enlarge the whole display (Full-Screen Zoom) or a specific window inside the display (Window Zoom). In addition, VoiceOver is compatible with Zoom.

An iPhone shows the Zoom menu.

Prepare Zoom

1. Zoom may be activated from the Settings > Accessibility menu.
2. The following may be modified:
   - Focus on what you're doing and see where your cursor is as you type.
   - When a keyboard appears, Smart Typing automatically switches to Window Zoom.

- Zoom may be managed by shortcuts on a separate keyboard.
- Adjust the Zoom Controller's hue and transparency in addition to activating its other controls.
- There are two zoom regions available: the whole screen and the window.
- Zoom Filter Options: Low Light, Grayscale, Inverted Grayscale, and None.
- Adjust the maximum zoom by dragging the slider.

3. The following options appear underneath Pointer Control on the iPhone while you're using a pointer device.

- Zoom Pan lets you customize how the on-screen content shifts when you move the mouse. You may choose between Continuous, Centered, or Edges.
- Scale the pointer up or down as you zoom in and out.

4. Settings > Accessibility > Accessibility Shortcut > Zoom to add Zoom as an accessibility shortcut.

Activate Zoom

1. You can activate Zoom by using a three-finger double-tap on the screen, or by using the Accessibility Shortcut.

2. Do one of the following to see more of the display:
   - To change the magnification, touch the screen twice with three fingers (without raising any of your fingers between taps) and drag in either direction. A third option is to use three fingers to touch and hold, and then move the Zoom Level slider.
   - To control the zoom, click and drag the Zoom lever at the bottom of the window.
   - Use three fingers to drag the screen.
3. Zoom menu settings may be changed by using a three-finger touch to access the menu, and then adjusting the following options:
   - Pick Your Area: You may either zoom in on a window or the whole screen.
   - Adjustable Zoom in/out (Window) Select Resize Lens and then use the circular handles to reposition the lens.
   - Pick Your Filter: Low Light, Grayscale, Inverted Grayscale, or Inverted.
   - Display Controls: Display the Zoom Slider.
4. The Zoom Controller may be used in a variety of ways:
   - A little tap on the controller will do.
   - Double-tap the controller to zoom in or out.
   - Zoom in and drag the controller to the pan.

Zooming in and out with the Magic Keyboard always keeps the insertion point in the exact center of the display.

Double-tapping the screen with three fingers, or using the Accessibility Shortcut, will disable Zoom.

Adjust the Color Scheme For Better Readability

To better view what's on your iPhone's screen, you may invert colors, filter them, and even make translucent elements solid.

Use the brightness slider in the Control Center for a quick adjustment.

Flip The Hues

The iPhone's screen may have its colors inverted to make reading simpler. This is particularly helpful for software and websites that do not have a "Dark Mode" option.

1. To adjust the display and text size, go to Settings > Accessibility.
2. Colors are inverted intelligently outside of photos.
   - Traditional inverting causes the screen's colors to be inverted.

Use A Color Filter To Modify Hues

1. To adjust the display and text size, go to Settings > Accessibility.
2. Select Color Filters, switch on Color Filters, then select a color filter to apply it.

   You may modify the brightness or color by dragging the corresponding slider. The colored pencils show how the filter modifies various hues.

   Color filters may drastically alter the feel of a video or photo.

To lessen the impact of vivid hues, activate the Reduce White Point setting.

When it becomes dark outside, you may utilize Night Shift to make the colors on your screen seem more cozy. By default, Night Shift will undo any color inversions or filter effects (except grayscale).

Add Solidity To See-Through Objects

By default, certain backgrounds will seem hazy or translucent. By filling them with a solid color, these translucent backgrounds become opaque. By doing so, you may make certain sections of your screen more minimalistic and therefore more legible.

1. To adjust the display and text size, go to Settings > Accessibility.
2. Reduce Transparency must be activated.

Separate without the use of color

The hue of some screen elements is used to denote vital information. You may use other distinguishing features, such as shapes or text, instead.

1. To adjust the display and text size, go to Settings > Accessibility.
2. Activate the color-free differentiation feature.

For on/off controls, use ones and zeros.

When a switch is activated, it will glow green. You may also use the numbers "1" and "0" for on and off, respectively, on switches.

1. To adjust the display and text size, go to Settings > Accessibility.
2. Switch on the On/Off Tags.

Improve The Readability Of Text

If you want to make text on your iPhone easier to read, you may adjust its weight, size, and darkness. Text that can be tapped on may also be highlighted.

A quick font size adjustment may be made by adding the feature to Control Center.

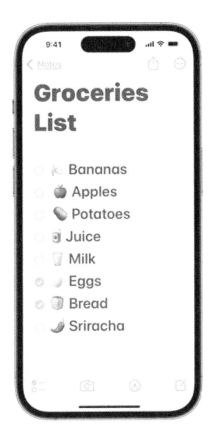

A bulleted list in Notes with the font size and color changed to accommodate those with visual impairments, and the button shapes activated.

Improve Readability Of Content

Apps like Settings, Calendar, Contacts, Mail, Messages, and Notes that enable Dynamic Type allow you to customize font weight, size, and darkness to your liking.

1. To adjust the display and text size, go to Settings > Accessibility.
2. Try one of the following:
   - Expand font size: Select Larger font, then increase or decrease the font size using the slider (enable Larger Accessibility Sizes to see other possibilities).
     You may alternatively navigate to Settings > Display & Brightness > Display Zoom, then choose Larger Text to view larger buttons.
   - Make it stand out more by activating Bold Text.
   - Render text darker: Turn on Increase Contrast to boost readability by making the text stand out more.
   - If you enable Button Shapes, any text that triggers an action when you touch it will be highlighted.

Zoom lets you magnify content on the screen, while Magnifier lets you do the same thing with physical letters.

Increase Or Decrease The Font Size
1. Open Control Center and then press the font Size button to increase or decrease the font size in the current app.

(Insert Text Size by going to Settings > Control Center and tapping the Insert button next to Text Size if you don't see it there.)

2. To adjust the font size, use the up and down arrows on the slider.

Select All Apps from the bottom of the screen to adjust the font size for all installed programs.

If you're having problems locating the pointer on the screen when using a mouse or other device with an onscreen pointer, you may increase its size.

Dial 911 On Your iPhone

During an emergency, dial 911 on your iPhone by pressing the SOS button.

If you have an iPhone and cellular service is available, you may use it to easily contact rescue workers and inform others you've designated to support you in an emergency.

If you have an iPhone 14 or later (of any model), you may be able to make a satellite call to 911 even if you don't have mobile coverage.

Quickly Dial 911

Quickly dial 911 (in any country or area other than India).

- Hold the side button and either volume button at the same time until the sliders display and the Emergency SOS countdown expires, then let go of the buttons.

Or, you may configure your iPhone to launch Emergency SOS when you swiftly push the side button five times. To activate Call with 5 Presses, go to the menu and choose Emergency SOS.

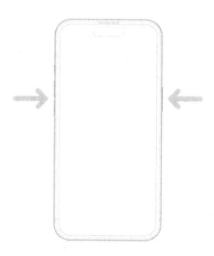

Symbol of an iPhone with arrows indicating the side button and the left and right volume controls.

Unless you cancel, your iPhone will send a text message to your emergency contacts once an emergency call finishes. Your iPhone broadcasts your current location (if available) and—for some time after you activate SOS mode—your emergency contacts get updates when your location changes.

In an emergency, dial 911 immediately (in India).

- Press the side button three times in rapid succession to bring up the sliders and terminate the Emergency SOS countdown.
- Hold the side button and either volume button until the sliders display and the Emergency SOS countdown expires, then release the buttons to activate the Accessibility Shortcut.

iPhones, by default, will sound an alarm, begin a countdown, and then dial 911.

Unless you cancel, your iPhone will send a text message to your emergency contacts once an emergency call finishes. Your iPhone broadcasts your current location (if available) and—for some time after you activate SOS mode—your emergency contacts get updates when your location changes.

When your iPhone is locked, dial 911.

1. Emergency may be accessed via the Passcode screen.
2. Tap the Call button, then dial the appropriate emergency number (in the US, this would be 911).

Send An Urgent Message

1. Select the To box under Messages and enter 911 or your area's emergency number.
2. Make an urgent message by typing.
3. Select the "Send" button.

You need to modify your SOS emergency settings.

1. Just choose "Emergency SOS" from the "Settings" menu.
2. Take any of these actions:
   - Activate or deactivate "Call with Hold and Release" Hold and release the side and volume buttons to start a countdown to summon emergency assistance.
   - Disable or enable "Call with 5 presses" To initiate a 911 call, quickly push the side button five times.
   - Keep track of your important phone numbers: In Health, hit Set Up Emergency Contacts or Edit Emergency Contacts.

You may not be able to make an emergency call from your iPhone if it is not active, if it is not compatible with or set to function on a specific cellular network, if your iPhone does not have a SIM card, or if your SIM card is locked with a PIN.

- When you place an emergency call in certain countries or locations, emergency personnel may be able to obtain your location data (if it is determinable).
- Learn the restrictions of making emergency calls via Wi-Fi by reading your carrier's emergency calling information.
- With CDMA, after an emergency call ends, the iPhone enters emergency call mode for a few minutes to enable a callback from emergency services. Data transfer and texting are disabled at this time.
- To facilitate a comeback from emergency services, it is common practice to temporarily deactivate call features that block or quiet incoming calls after an emergency call has been placed. Screen time, Do Not Disturb, and Silence Unknown Calls are all examples.
- Any incoming calls (including those from emergency services) on a Dual SIM iPhone that has Wi-Fi Calling disabled will be sent to voicemail (if your carrier offers this feature) and you will not get missed call alerts.
- When a line is busy or out of service, you may prevent calls from going to voicemail by setting up conditional call forwarding (if supported by your carrier).

- Data transmission via USB 3 and DisplayPort connections will be unavailable while using an iPhone equipped with a USB-C connector and a suitable accessory for up to 5 minutes after the conclusion of an emergency session (call or text). The exact timing changes depending on where you are. After this time has elapsed, you will need to unplug and reconnect your device to resume utilizing your accessory. The charging process will proceed as normal.

Emergency SOS On Your iPhone

When you are outside of your mobile phone and Wi-Fi connection, you may still text emergency services with the help of Emergency SOS on your iPhone 14 or later (of any model).

Not all nations or areas provide the emergency SOS via satellite service.

Ahead Of Leaving Cell And Wi-Fi Service

Prepare for a trip where you may not have access to cellular or Wi-Fi networks by making a Medical ID, adding emergency contacts, and testing out the Emergency SOS demo.

1. Just choose "Emergency SOS" from the "Settings" menu.

2. Just touch the link below and scroll down Check Out This Sample.

Calling 911 is not part of the Emergency SOS demo.

Use Your iPhone's Satellite Connection

Use your iPhone's satellite connection to get in touch with Emergency SOS.

You can utilize Emergency SOS via satellite if you need help from 911 but don't have a mobile phone or Wi-Fi coverage.

1. Try phoning 911 or emergency services. The iPhone will still try to make the 911 call using other networks if they are available, even if your regular cellular carrier network is down.
2. If you are unable to make a voice call, you may send a text to emergency services by selecting "Emergency Text via Satellite." Another option is to open the Messages app, type 911 or SOS into the text field, and then choose Emergency Services.
3. Select "Report Emergency" and proceed with the on-screen prompts.

The Emergency SOS display verifies the phone's connectivity and urges the user to maintain satellite orientation. A button labeled "Opening Messages" may be found toward the base of your display.

Make sure your phone has a clean line of sight to the sky by holding it naturally in your hand; there's no need to elevate your arm or hold the phone aloft. It might be difficult to establish a connection with a satellite when you are surrounded by thick vegetation or other obstacles.

Once you're linked up, your iPhone will begin a text conversation in which it will relay important details such as your Medical ID and emergency contact information (if you've set them up), your responses to the emergency questionnaire, your position (including elevation), and the status of your iPhone's battery. You have the option of including your emergency contacts in the message you send to 911.

Chapter Two

Create And Review Your Health Card

Allergies, medical problems, and emergency contacts are just some of the pieces of information that might be included on a medical ID. If you activate Emergency SOS via satellite, your emergency contacts will be contacted and your iPhone or Apple Watch will show this information to the person helping you.

Put Together A Health Card

Use the Health app to create a Medical ID.

1. Get out your iPhone's Health app.
2. Select your photo in the upper right corner, then select Medical ID.
3. Enter your details under Get Started or Edit.
4. Select Add Emergency Contact under Emergency Contacts.

Unless you cancel, your iPhone will send a text message to your emergency contacts once an emergency call finishes. Your iPhone broadcasts your current location (if available) and—for some time after you activate SOS mode—your emergency contacts get updates when your location changes.

5. Choose the Done option.

From the Home screen, you may access your Medical ID by touching and holding the Health app icon and then selecting Medical ID.

Provide Your Medical Identification Provide your medical identification to emergency personnel.

Your Medical ID shows on the Lock Screen of your iPhone and Apple Watch, and it may be immediately shared during an emergency call (in the United States and Canada).

1. Get out your iPhone's Health app.
2. Select your photo in the upper right corner, then select Medical ID.
3. Select "Edit," "Show When Locked," and "Emergency Call" from the list of options at the bottom.

In an emergency, first responders may access your Medical ID by sliding up or pushing the Home button (depending on your iPhone model), selecting Emergency on the password screen, and then selecting Medical ID from the Unlock screen.

Use The Built-In Check-In Feature

Use the iPhone's built-in Check-In feature to broadcast your location to your pals.

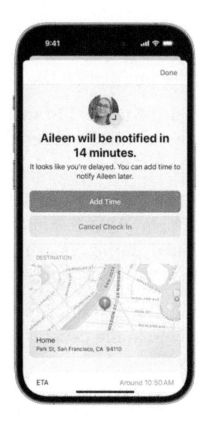

A buddy will be alerted in 14 minutes, and there are buttons to either extend the period or cancel the Check-In below the timer. A map of the current location is shown at the bottom.

To use Check-In, both the sender and the receiver must be running iOS 17. Due to local regulations, location sharing is currently unavailable in South Korea and may be so in other countries as well.

Check-In Procedure

If you don't successfully finish your Check In, your iPhone will automatically alert a friend that it has arrived, and you may decide what information they will view.

If a buddy sends you a Check-In but you haven't received your iPhone yet, you can still see where they are, how much battery life they have left, what kind of cellular coverage they have, and more.

Deliver Check-in

1. Launch the iPhone's Messages application.
2. Select a discussion from the drop-down menu or tap the Compose button to start a new message.
3. Select Apps, then More, then Check-In, and finally Edit.
   - Time I'll Get There: Enter your starting location, mode of transportation (driving, public transportation, or walking), and final destination. If your iPhone hasn't moved forward in its trip after a certain amount of time, or if it hasn't arrived at its destination, Check In will alert your buddy. After a successful arrival, the Check-In process

concludes and your buddy is alerted that your iPhone has arrived.

- If you're meeting someone for the first time, provide an exact time. Check-In will alert your buddy if you don't finish the check-in by the time you specified.

4. Choose the Send option.

If your iPhone doesn't reach its destination or if you don't cancel the Check-In and answer the Check-In prompts, your buddy will get information on your iPhone's travel.

Your check-in recipient may get delayed or early notice and the ability to see the iPhone data you provided with them if you start a Check-In and subsequently lose service or your iPhone switches down.

Extend Your Check-In Time

If you need more time, you may extend the time to your Check-In.

1. Launch the iPhone's Messages application.
2. Check-in with a buddy and then initiate a discussion with them.
3. Select an option from the Check-In message's Details menu, then hit Add Time.

To revoke a Check-In

If you've finished your trip, or you wish to terminate your session for whatever reason, you may cancel your Check In to let your buddy know.

1. Launch the iPhone's Messages application.
2. Check-in with a buddy and then initiate a discussion with them.
3. To cancel a check-in, choose Details from the Check-In message, then Cancel Check-In.

Pick Which Information To Reveal

You have the option to modify the information you provide a buddy during a Check-In.

1. Choose Conversations > Preferences.
2. Navigate down and choose Check In Information.
3. If you fail to complete your Check-In on time, you may decide what information to disclose.
   - Restricted: Tell others where you are and how much juice your iPhone and Apple Watch have left.
   - Full: Tell others where you are, how strong your signal is, how much juice you have left, how long it took you to get here, and when you last unlocked your iPhone or took off your Apple Watch.

Control Crash Reporting

The meaning of "Crash Detection"

Any iPhone 14 or later model may assist in linking you to emergency services and inform emergency contacts if it detects a major automobile collision.

Methods Of Accident Detection

When your iPhone detects a major automobile collision, it will show an alarm and will automatically begin an emergency phone call after 20 seconds unless you cancel. If your iPhone detects that you have been in a serious collision and you are unresponsive, it will play an audio message for emergency personnel detailing the nature of the accident, your precise location, and the approximate search radius.

Crash Detection will not supersede preexisting emergency calls when an accident is detected.

The iPhone will use Emergency SOS to make satellite calls to emergency services if you are involved in a serious vehicle accident and unresponsive and you are somewhere without cellular or Wi-Fi coverage.

Toggle Accident Reporting

Accident Reporting is enabled by default. Settings > Emergency SOS > Call After serious collision will disable Apple's automated emergency calls and notifications in the event of a serious automobile collision. Even if you haven't registered any third-party applications to get crash notifications, your smartphone will still alert them.

In case you have Apple products like CarPlay or an Apple Watch

When an iPhone with Crash Detection enabled is synced with a car running CarPlay, the iPhone will be used to contact emergency services in the event of a collision.

If you have your Apple Watch on at the time of an accident, your iPhone will handle calling for help, but your Apple Watch will handle the Crash Detection functions.

Use The Virtual Keyboard To Input Text

The iPhone's on-screen keyboard may be used for both typing and editing.

The iPhone's Magic Keyboard and Dictation are also available for text entry.

Type In Your Message

Use the on-screen keyboard to type in your message.

Tapping a text field in any program that supports it will bring up the onscreen keyboard. You may type by tapping individual keys, or you can utilize QuickPath (not available for all languages) to enter a word by sliding from one letter to the next without raising your finger. To finish a word, raise your finger. You can switch between the two while typing, and you may do so at any time throughout a phrase. (The whole word is erased if you touch the Delete key after using the slide method of typing.)

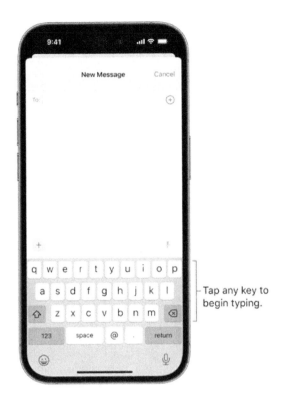

The Mail app is now displaying a blank email. The virtual keyboard appears in the screen's lower half.

- Slide to an uppercase letter by touching or tapping the Shift key.
- To activate Caps Lock, press the Shift key twice.
- Put a period and a space at the end of a phrase quickly: Just hit the Space bar twice in a row.
- Fill in the blanks with digits and punctuation: You may use the numeric keypad or the symbol keypad.

- You may undo autocorrect by tapping the underlined word and then tapping the spelling you wish to use. As you write, incorrect words are automatically fixed and momentarily underlined so you know what has been altered.
- Tap the red highlighted misspelled word to view potential fixes; tap a suggestion to replace the misspelled word, or input the correction yourself.
- Cancel the current change: Use three fingers to swipe left, then choose Undo from the main menu.
- Use a three-finger swipe to the right and the Undo button at the top of the screen to undo the previous change.

Activate The Haptic And Audio Feedback

Activate the haptic and audio feedback on your keyboard.

The tapping of the keyboard may be heard or felt, depending on your preferences.

1. To adjust the keyboard's feedback, choose Sounds & Haptics > Settings.
2. Sounds and Haptics allows you to hear and feel tapping while typing.

Make The Virtual Keyboard Into A Mouse

To more easily move and put the insertion point, you may transform the virtual keyboard into a trackpad.

Slide your finger over the keyboard to move the insertion point.

The Notes app is currently processing a document. Trackpad mode has been activated for the on-screen keyboard located in the lower half of the display.

1. To make the keyboard go from white to light gray, press and hold the Space bar with one finger.

2. You may slide your finger around the keyboard to change the insertion place.

   To make a selection, tap and hold a key with a second finger, then move your first finger across the keyboard to pick the desired text.

Use Accents Or Diacritical Marks

Type in special characters such as accents or diacritical marks.

To create a certain character on the keyboard, press and hold the key that corresponds to that character.

Entering é, for instance, requires touching and holding the e key, gliding your finger over the keyboard, and then releasing it on the desired choice.

When you press and hold the E key on the virtual keyboard, more accented characters will emerge.

The following are additional options:

- Touch and hold the corresponding Arabic number on a Thai keyboard to access the corresponding Thai numeral.
- Tap a recommended character or candidate at the top of the keyboard to input it, or swipe left to view additional choices when using a Chinese, Japanese, or Arabic keypad.

- Please press the right-most-up arrow to see all available options. Select the down arrow to go back to the first list.

Replace Text

1. Choose the words you wish to shift in your text editor of choice.
2. You may move the highlighted text throughout the app by touching and holding it until it pops up.

The Notes app is currently processing a document. The virtual keyboard appears in the screen's lower half. The goal is to reposition some of the content inside the document.

If you change your mind about moving the text, raise your finger before dragging, or moving the text off the screen.

Use The Advanced Typing Options

Predictive text and auto-correction are only two of the advanced typing options that may be toggled on and off.

1. Touch and hold the Next Keyboard Emoji key or the Switch Keyboard key while typing on the on-screen keyboard, and then choose Keyboard Settings from the menu that appears. Alternative: go to Settings > General > Keyboard.
2. Make changes to the keyboard settings (below All Keyboards) by clicking the green On button.

One-Handed Typing

If you want to type with only one hand, you may make the keys more accessible to your thumb.

Three options—English (US), Emoji, and Keyboard Feedback—appear in the Keyboard Settings panel. You may choose between left-handed, default, and right-handed layouts using the buttons at the very bottom of the menu. This page's default layout has been chosen.

1. Select the desired emoji by touching and holding the Next Keyboard Emoji or Switch Keyboard key.
2. Select a keyboard layout by tapping it. To make the keyboard appear on the right-hand side of the

display, for instance, choose the Right-Handed Layout option.

A touch on the keyboard's right or left edge will reset it to its middle position.

Type Using iPhone Dictation

You can use the iPhone's Dictation feature to dictate text in any app that supports typing. You can also use typing and Dictation together—the keyboard remains open during Dictation so you can effortlessly switch between voice and touch to input text. Touch-selectable text may be replaced by speech, for instance.

You can use your smartphone independently of an internet connection to handle dictation requests in a variety of languages. Dictated text may be communicated to the search provider when using a voice-activated search box.

Not all nations or areas have the same set of dictation functions, and not all languages support dictation.

Cellular data fees may apply while utilizing Dictation.

Engage Dictation

1. Select "Keyboard" under "General" under "Settings."
2. Activate the Dictation feature. If prompted, choose the dictation option.

Provide A Script

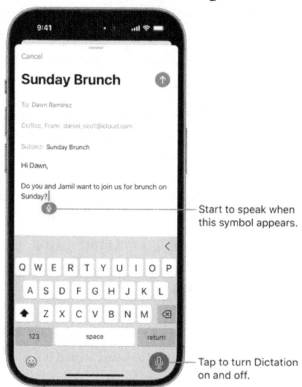

Start to speak when this symbol appears.

Tap to turn Dictation on and off.

The Mail app on-screen keyboard is now visible. A dictation button displays below the cursor in the text field once you click the Dictation button in the lower right corner of the screen.

44

1. If you wish to start dictating text, tap in the text area to set the insertion point.
2. When the on-screen keyboard (or a text field) displays a Dictate button, tap it.
3. Start dictating as soon as the Dictate button flashes into view next to the insertion point in the text field.
4. Simple formatting chores, such as adding an emoji or punctuation mark, may be accomplished by any of the following:
   - Spell out an emoji's name, such as "heart emoji" or "smiley face emoji."
   - The punctuation mark should be referred to by its proper name, such as "exclamation point."

   Dictation will automatically add commas, periods, and question marks to your text in the languages it supports. Settings > General > Keyboard is where you'll find the option to disable auto-punctuation.

   - Let's use a common formatting instruction, like "new line" or "new paragraph."
5. Tap the Dictate button after you're finished, otherwise Dictation will end after 30 seconds of silence.

Dictation may be used in any language for which a keyboard exists. See Add or change keyboards on iPhone.

1. Select "Keyboard" under "General" under "Settings."
2. It's time to disable dictation.

Text Selection, Editing, And Use

Text fields in iPhone applications may be selected and edited using the on-screen keyboard.

Pick Your Words

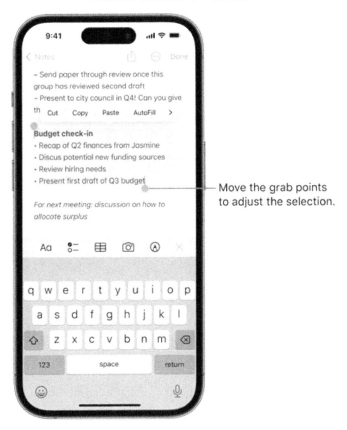

Move the grab points to adjust the selection.

The Notes app's text selection feature is used. The options to Cut, Copy, Paste and Autofill are located just above the highlighted text. The highlighted text has grab points at its beginning and conclusion, so you can easily move the selection around.

1. Do one of the following to choose text:
   - Tap twice with a single finger.

- Choose a Paragraph Tap three times with a single finger.
- Click on a section of text: To pick text in a block, double-tap and hold the first word, then drag the grab points.

2. Select the text you wish to modify, then either enter directly into the box or press the selection to bring up a menu of editing options:
   - To make a clean cut, use a tap cut or a two-finger squeeze to close.
   - Copy: Tap Copy or squeeze closed with three fingers.
   - A three-finger squeeze or a tap on Paste will open it.
   - Choose All Choose all of the current text.
   - Look at recommended other text or have Siri propose new wording.
   - Style: Apply a style to the chosen text.
   - Press the Next Page button Explore further.

You may drag the chosen text to a new spot without having to cut or copy it first.

Type In New Text Or Make Changes

1. Any of the following may be used to set the insertion point at the location where you'll be writing or editing:

- Simply tap the area where you'd want to type new content.
- Magnify the text by touching and holding it, and then drag the insertion point to a new location.

A notation indicating the location of the insertion point inside the document. The text around the insertion point is enlarged to aid in precise placement.

To modify specific sections of text in a lengthy document, touch and hold the right border of the page, then move the scroller.

2. Simply enter or copy and paste the relevant content.

Using Universal Clipboard, you can cut or copy text from one Apple device and paste it into a text editor on another.

Utilize The Predictive Text Capabilities

The predictive text allows you to type and finish full phrases with a few touches. Words, emoticons, and suggested information appear as you write on the iPhone keyboard (not accessible in all languages). When you write anything like this in Messages, for instance:

- Type "I'm at" followed by a space, and the option to choose your current location will display.
- Word and phrase completion suggestions appear inline as you type.

Make Use Of Text Prediction In Real Time

Word and phrase completion suggestions display inline as you write in gray. If you want to use the suggested word or phrase, use the Space bar; if not, keep typing.

If you accept an inline prediction and then change your mind, touch the Delete key, and then tap the word you were in the middle of typing.

Your language may not allow inline predictive text.

Use Text Prediction

You may use the on-screen keyboard normally, and suggestions for words, emoji, and information will show above it as you enter.

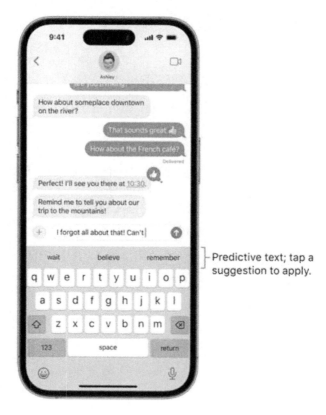

Predictive text; tap a suggestion to apply.

The Messages app's on-screen keyboard is now visible. As you type into the text box, recommendations for the following word will appear above the keyboard.

A space will be added after the recommended term if you want to use it. The space behind a comma, period, or other punctuation mark is removed mechanically.

Tap the choice inside quote marks to choose your original term and delete the recommendations.

Switch Off The Text Predictor

1. While typing, hold the Next, Emoji, or Switch keys.
2. To disable Predictive Typing, choose Keyboard Settings.

Turning off Predictive may not prevent the iPhone from trying to repair misspelled words. To accept a change, just hit Return or type a space. To reject a correction, hit the "x." The iPhone will cease making the same recommendation once it has been declined many times.

When you disable Predictive, it stops predicting both the main text and the inline content.

Chapter Three

Write And Draw In Documents

The markup on the iPhone allows you to write and draw in documents.

You may use the Markup tools to draw and sketch documents in compatible applications including Mail, Messages, Notes, and Photos. The Markup tools may also be used to annotate screenshots, PDFs, and other document types.

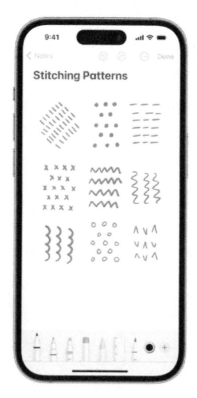

The Notes app has been launched, and the Markup toolbar has appeared on the screen's bottom. From left to right, you can see the Color Picker and the Add button, as well as the Pen, Mono line, Marker, Eraser, Lasso, Ruler, and Pencil that make up the Markup tools.

Sketch And Jot Down

1. Select Markup from the menu in a compatible app.
2. In the Markup toolbar, touch the pen, marker, or pencil tool, then write or draw with your finger.

Try any of the following while sketching:

- Alter the line's density: To change settings, hit the toolbar's drawing tool of choice and then tap the gear icon.
- Modify the level of transparency: Drag the slider after tapping the desired drawing tool from the toolbar.
- Alter the hue: To fine-tune your color selection, hit the Color Picker icon on the toolbar and then the Grid, Spectrum, or Sliders buttons.
- To undo it, select it and then click the Undo button.

- Take a ruler and draw a line: Select the ruler tool from the menu bar, and then draw a line parallel to the ruler's length.
  - Simply touch and hold the ruler with two fingers, then spin your fingers to adjust the angle.
  - Simply drag the ruler with one finger to move it without affecting the angle.
  - To dismiss the ruler, just press its icon again on the toolbar.
3. You may dismiss the Markup toolbar by selecting Markup or Done from its menu.

Remove An Error

In a compatible app, choose the eraser icon from the Markup toolbar and do one of the following actions:

- Use your finger as a pixel eraser and rub over the error to get rid of it.
- Use your finger as an eraser and touch the thing to erase it.
- You may use the pixel and object erasers interchangeably. Select Pixel Eraser or Object Eraser by tapping the eraser tool one more.

If you don't see the Markup toolbar, hit the Markup button or Markup. Tap the collapsed toolbar if it is present.

Markup Object Relocation

1. In the Markup toolbar, press the lasso tool (between the eraser and ruler tools), then use your finger to drag around the items you wish to move.

   If you're using a compatible app and don't see the Markup toolbar, choose the Markup button or Markup. Tap the collapsed toolbar if it is present.

2. Raise a finger.
3. Drag and drop the chosen item by touching it with your finger.
4. You may disable the lasso by tapping the screen.

Annotate Photographs And Documents

Markup tools allow you to annotate photographs and documents with text, shapes, signatures, stickers, and image descriptions in applications that enable this feature.

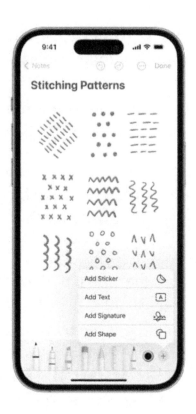

The Add button in the Notes app's bottom-right corner is chosen, and the Markup toolbar opens at the note's bottom. The following choices are accessible in the Add menu: Add Sticker, Add Text, Add Signature, and Add Shape.

Insert Text

1. Select Markup from the menu in a compatible app.
2. Add Text by tapping the Add button in the Markup toolbar.

3. Use the keyboard to type into the text field after tapping it.
4. Use the font, size, justification, style, and color pickers at the screen's bottom.
5. Select the More menu to edit the text box by cutting, copying, duplicating, or erasing it.
6. Tap anywhere outside the text area when you're finished.
7. You may dismiss the Markup toolbar by selecting Markup or Done from its menu.

Include A Form

1. Select Markup from the menu in a compatible app.
2. Select the desired shape by tapping the Add button located in the Markup toolbar.
3. To insert a shape, tap the desired icon and then perform one of the following:
   - Drag the shape to reposition it.
   - To adjust the size of the shape, drag any of the dots around the form's border.
   - Modify the orientation or size of the shape: Select any green dot and move it along the form's border.
   - Select a Markup tool from the menu.

- Prepare a copy, distribute it, or get rid of it: Select a choice by tapping the More button in the shape's menu.
4. When you're satisfied with the form, press the screen to save your changes.
5. Markup button or Done will dismiss the Markup toolbar.

Make A Squiggle

For usage in diagrams and drawings, Markup allows you to create perfectly straight lines, curved lines, and other geometric forms.

1. Tap the Markup button or Markup in a compatible app, and then choose a pen or highlighter from the Markup toolbar.
2. Create a form by tracing it with your finger once, and then stopping.

   The sketch is instantly replaced with a precise replica of the form. (Hit Undo if you want to maintain the scribbled outline.)

Lines, arrows, arcs, continuous lines with right angles, squares, circles, rectangles, triangles, pentagons, chat bubbles, hearts, stars, and clouds are all within your reach.

Add Signature

1. Select the Markup button or Markup inside an app that supports it.
2. Add then Add Signature may be found in the Markup toolbar.
3. Sign your name with a finger.
   To start again, use the Clear button and then sign your name again.
4. Once you've tapped "Done," you may make any of the following changes:
   - Please re-sign here: Pull it.
   - Drag any dot along the signature's outline to resize it.
   - Alter the signature's line thickness and color as needed: Select a Markup tool from the menu.
   - Prepare a copy, distribute it, or get rid of it: To change your signature, touch the More button that appears next to the signature.
5. When you're finished making changes to the signature, tap anywhere outside the box.

Sign In And Edit Signatures

The signature you make on an iPhone is stored and may be used again once you press Add Signature. You may create several signatures, such as a nickname or initials, and erase signatures.

1. Select the Markup button or Markup inside an app that supports it.
2. Add then Add Signature may be found in the Markup toolbar.
3. To add a signature, choose Add or Remove Signature and then press the Add button.
4. Select the desired signature format (full name, alias, or initials) by tapping the arrow next to New Signature.
5. Sign with your finger and press the Done button.

Select the signature you want to remove, then hit the Delete button. Select the signatures you wish to remove by tapping Add or Remove Signature and then selecting the Delete option.

Sticker it and Mark it Up!

Markup allows you to decorate documents and photos with stickers from your library.

1. Select the Markup button or Markup inside an app that supports it.
2. To insert a sticker, select it and touch the Add button in the Markup toolbar.
3. Just tap and drag a sticker onto your paper or picture.
   Before raising your finger, you may tweak the sticker's angle by rotating a second finger around it.

4. To resize an existing sticker, tap and drag a dot inside its border.

The App Store offers downloadable sticker sets. Stickers may be made in the Messages app, and images or Live Photos can be used as inspiration.

Describe pictures in your own words
Markup allows you to annotate pictures in applications like Photos. When you use the Image Explorer, VoiceOver will read out loud the labels you provide.

1. Select Markup from the menu in a compatible app.
2. Select Description from the Markup toolbar's Add button.
3. Enter your description, then hit Done.

Modify Your iPhone's Volume

When you're on the phone or listening to music, movies, or other media on an iPhone, you may use the buttons on the side of your smartphone to control the audio level. Aside from that, the buttons adjust the level of the device's ringer, alerts, and any other audible effects. Siri also has the capability of adjusting the volume.

If you want to adjust the volume, just tell Siri, "Turn up the volume" or "Turn down the volume."

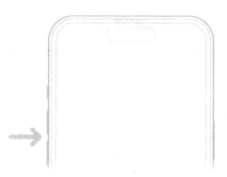

The left-hand side of the top of your iPhone is where the volume controls are located.

The ringer and alert volumes may be locked under Settings.

1. Choose Preferences.
2. Tap audio/haptics.
3. Switch off Button Change.

Change The Settings Under The Settings Menu

You can change the volume in the Control Center whether your iPhone is locked or you're using an app.

To adjust the volume, launch Control Center and use the slider.

Mute The Sound Of Your Headphones

1. Choose Options > Sounds & Haptics > Headphone Safety.
2. Turn on Reduce Loud Sounds, then move the slider to determine the maximum level.

The Reduce Loud Sounds setting may be locked in place when you set up Screen Time for a family member. Turn on Content & Privacy Restrictions by going to Settings > Screen Time > Content & Privacy Restrictions > Reduce Loud Sounds, then tapping Reduce Loud Sounds and choosing Don't Allow.

Put calls, alerts, and notifications on hold for the time being.

To enable Do Not Disturb mode, launch the Control Center, choose Focus, and finally select the option.

Turn iPhone To Vibrate-Only Mode

To activate Silent mode on an iPhone, flip the Ring/Silent switch to the orange position (this may vary by model). Simply turning the switch off will restore normal operation.

Silent mode may be activated on the iPhone 15 Pro and 15 Pro Max by navigating to Settings > Sounds & Haptics > Silent.

The Ring/Silent toggle has been replaced on the iPhone 15 Pro and 15 Pro Max with an Action button. The Action button may be used to toggle Silent mode on or off, in addition to other purposes.

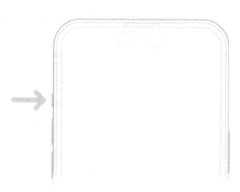

A close-up of the top left corner of the iPhone's front panel, where the Ring/Silent switch is located above the volume controls.

When the iPhone's Silent mode is off, all audio is played. With Silent mode on, your iPhone will not make any audible notifications or noises of any kind (but it may still vibrate).

Notifications like the clock, music applications, and many games still use the built-in speaker even when Silent mode is activated. The Camera, Voice Memo, and Emergency Alert sounds may play even when the Ring/mute switch is in the mute position in specific nations or areas.

Many volume controls on the iPhone may help prevent damage to your hearing from using headphones at high volumes.

Launch iPhone Applications

Apps may be launched instantly from the Home Screen or the App Library.

1. Swipe up from the bottom of the screen (on a Face ID iPhone) or click the Home button (on a non-Face ID iPhone) to access the Home Screen.

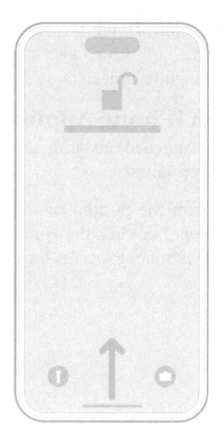

An example of the Home Screen is accessed by swiping up from the bottom of the screen.

2. To see other app pages on the Home Screen, swipe left.

This diagram demonstrates how to access additional Home Screen pages containing applications by sliding left.

3. Swipe left past all your Home Screen pages to view App Library, where your applications are arranged by category.
4. Activate a program by touching its icon.
5. Swipe up from the bottom of the screen (on a Face ID iPhone) or click the Home button (on a non-Face ID iPhone) to access the App Switcher again.

Apps May Be Located In The App Library

App Library presents your applications sorted into categories, such as Social, Entertainment, Productivity, and finance. The applications you use the most are prioritized and placed at the highest level in their respective categories, making them quick and easy to find and launch.

The iPhone's app collection is broken down into categories like "Utilities," "Social," "Entertainment," and so on.

The applications in App Library are automatically sorted into groups by category depending on how you often use them. Apps in the App Library may be added to the Home Screen, but cannot be relocated inside the App Library.

Browse the available apps and launch one
1. To access the App Library, launch the Home Screen and swipe left to get past all the Home Screen pages.
2. You can find the app you're searching for by tapping the search bar at the top of the screen and typing its name. You may also use the scroll bar to go through the alphabetical list.
3. Tap the app icon to launch it.

If a category includes a few tiny app icons, you may press them to expand the category and view all the applications in it.

Display Or Hide Apps From Home Screen
Because you can locate all of your applications in the App Library, you may not need as many Home Screen pages for apps. By hiding a few pages, you may move the App Library to the first page on your Home Screen. (The secret pages may be revealed whenever you choose.)

1. The applications on the Home Screen will bounce if you touch and hold the screen for a while.
2. Click the dots in the lower-right corner of the screen.
   Your Home Screen pages are shown as thumbnails with checkboxes underneath them.
3. Remove the checkmarks with a touch to make the pages invisible.
   Tap the checkboxes to reveal the hidden pages.
4. If using Face ID, tap Done; otherwise, touch the Home button.

When you hide the other Home Screen pages, it just takes one or two swipes to go from the first Home Screen page to the App Library (and back).

Any newly downloaded applications from the App Store may be placed in the App Library rather than the Home Screen if the Home Screen pages are hidden.

Sort The Apps On Your Home Screen

If you have many Home Screen pages, can adjust their order. If you want to prioritize the applications you use the most, you may create a page on your Home Screen dedicated to them.

1. To make the applications dance on the Home Screen, touch and hold the background.

2. Click the dots in the lower-right corner of the screen.

Your Home Screen pages are shown as thumbnails with checkboxes underneath them.

3. Simply tap and hold a page on the Home Screen, and then drag it to its new location.
4. If using Face ID, tap Done twice, otherwise, touch the Home button twice.

Newly acquired App Store downloads may be placed on either the Home Screen and App Library or just the App Library.

1. Select Home Screen > Settings.
2. You may decide whether new applications will be added to the Home Screen and the App Library, or only the App Library.

You must enable Show in App Library for app notification badges to show up in the App Library.

Copy an app's Home Screen shortcut from the App Library

If an app isn't currently on the Home Screen, you may add it from the App Library.

Touch and hold the app, then tap Add to Home Screen (accessible only if the app isn't already on the Home Screen).

Both the Home screen and the App Library will show the app.

Access Your Favorite Applications

When you power on or awaken your iPhone, you'll see the Lock Screen. You can access your favorite applications' information, manage media playback, use the camera and Control Center, and more, all without unlocking your phone.

You may customize your Lock Screen by picking a background, presenting a favorite picture, altering the typeface of the time, adding widgets, and more.

Time and date are shown toward the top of the iPhone Lock Screen, while the camera and flashlight symbols are located toward the bottom.

Access Several Settings And Functionalities
From the Lock Screen, you may access several settings and functionalities.

While the iPhone is locked, the Lock Screen provides rapid access to frequently used functions and information. The following actions may be performed from the Lock Screen:

- Swipe left to access the camera. Camera activation on compatible devices is as simple as touching and holding the button, and then lifting your finger.
- If you have an iPhone equipped with Face ID, you can access Control Center by swiping down from the top right corner of the screen; on other iPhones, you'll need to slide up from the bottom edge of the display.
- For prior announcements, please see: Just swipe up from the middle.
- Explore further widgets: To the right! Widgets on the Lock Screen and Home Screen may be used to conduct actions; for instance, you can press an item in the Reminders widget to mark it as completed, or you can hit the Play button in the Podcasts widget to begin playing an episode.
- Play, stop, rewind, and fast-forward media by tapping the playback controls (Now Playing) on the Lock Screen.

Exhibit sneak peeks at incoming notifications when locked in

1. Choose Notifications > Settings.
2. Select Always from the Show Previews menu.
3. Modify the Lock Screen notifications whatever you like:

- To see just the total count of alerts, choose Count.
- Check out the different stacks of alerts for each app: To stack, choose.
- Take a look at a rundown of the alerts: Check the List.

The Lock Screen notifications may be rearranged by pinching the screen.

Notification previews may contain text from Messages, lines from Mail messages, and data about Calendar invites.

Lock Screen Live Activity Monitoring and Management

Live Activities, such as sports scores, order statuses, and media playback, may be seen on the Lock Screen so you can keep up even if you can't watch the whole thing.

The iPhone's playback controls (Now Playing) may be accessed from the Lock Screen, allowing you to play, stop, rewind, and fast-forward music, movies, and other media.

The Lock Screen of your iPhone may also be used to manage media playing on a far-off gadget (such as an Apple TV or HomePod).

The music player's remote controls are shown on the Lock Screen with an album art cover.

Quickly Interact With Your iPhone

Quick action menus, previews, and other features may be accessed from the Home Screen, App Library, Control Center, and inside individual programs.

Access the App Drawer and Home Screen for instant results.

You may access the app's fast actions menu by touching and holding it anywhere on the Home Screen or in the App Library.

A blurred Home Screen, with the Camera fast actions menu appearing below the Camera app icon.

- Select Take Selfie by touching and holding the Camera.
- Keep your finger on the Maps icon until the menu appears, and then tap Send My Location.
- Select New Note by touching and holding Notes.

The applications will start to wiggle if you touch and hold one for too long before selecting a fast action. If Face ID isn't working, try pressing the Home button (or tapping Done) on your iPhone.

View previews and other menus with one-click options.

- A photo's context menu appears when you touch and hold it in Photos.
- You may preview the contents of a message and access a menu of actions by touching and holding it in your inbox in Mail.
- To access the menu, open Control Center and press and hold an item, such as the Camera button or the brightness slider.
- A notification may be dismissed from the Lock Screen by touching and holding it.
- To convert the virtual keyboard into a touchpad, tap and hold the Space bar with one finger while typing.

Utilizing Spotlight Search On An iPhone

Live Text on the iPhone allows you to search for text inside images, mail, messages, and contacts. You can check stock and currency information, and discover and access websites, applications, and photographs in your photo collection, across your system, and on the web.

App shortcuts for your most probable next action display in the Top Hit of a search. (When you look for "Photos," for instance, you'll get a link to your Favorites album.)

You may choose which applications appear in search results by going to Settings > Siri & Search. Search delivers recommendations based on your app use, and changes results as you enter.

Pick Which Programs To Index

1. To access Siri and Search, tap Settings.
2. To toggle the app's visibility in the search bar, scroll down and select the desired icon.

Do An iPhone Search

1. If your device has Face ID, you can access search by swiping down from the top of the Home or

Lock screen, or by tapping the Search icon at the bottom of the Home screen.

2. Simply type your query into the search bar.
3. Just choose one of the following:
   - Start your investigation by selecting Search or Go.
   - Get the recommended app and open it: You should use the app, so tap it.
   - Quickly respond by Running any shortcut, activating a timer, switching on a Focus, using Shazam to identify music, and more. Search for an app's name to find shortcuts available for the app, or make your own using the Shortcuts app.
   - Please visit the following website: Tap it.
   - Find out more about a suggested search by clicking on it: Select it, then select a result to open it.
   - Begin a brand-new lookup: Select the search field's Clear Text button.

Disable Personalized Nearby Recommendations

1. Enter Settings > Privacy & Security > Location Services.
2. To disable Suggestions & Search, go to System Services.

App-Based Searches

Many applications offer a search box or a search button so you can locate something inside the program. The Maps app, for instance, allows users to search for a certain address.

1. Select the app's search bar or button and type in your query.
   Swipe down from the top of the screen if you don't see a search bar or button.
2. Start typing, and then choose Search to search.

Include A Dictionary

You may expand the iPhone's search capabilities by installing a dictionary.

1. In the Menu, choose Settings > General > Dictionary.
2. Pick choose a reference book.

Modified Cellular Data Settings

The iPhone's cellular data settings may be seen and modified.

You can manage cellular data and roaming, choose which applications and services may use it, see your cellular data consumption, and adjust other settings.

Contact your wireless carrier if you have any questions or issues with your wireless plan, including but not limited to voicemail or billing.

The status bar on an iPhone displays an icon for the cellular data network if the device is connected to the internet via that network.

The GSM cellular networks that provide 5G, LTE, 4G, and 3G service all allow for simultaneous voice and data connections. If your iPhone doesn't have Wi-Fi, you can't access internet services on the go or during phone calls using any other cellular network. Depending on your network connection, you may not be able to accept calls when an iPhone transports data over the cellular network—when downloading a website, for example.

- In GSM networks, incoming calls may be sent to voicemail while using EDGE or GPRS for data transfers. When you receive and answer a call, your data transmission is temporarily halted.
- CDMA networks: On EV-DO connections, data transfers are halted while you answer incoming calls. Incoming calls on 1xRTT connections may be sent to voicemail while data is being transferred. When you receive and answer a call, your data transmission is temporarily halted.

When you hang up, data transmission will continue.

When Cellular Data is turned off, the device will rely only on Wi-Fi to send and receive data. Carrier fees may apply if you use cellular data. Siri and Messages are two examples of features and services that transmit data and may cause costs to your data plan.

Pick Your Cellular Data Plan

Pick your cellular data plan based on your needs in terms of data storage, speed, and battery life.

To switch Cellular Data on or off, click on Settings > Cellular.

When Cellular Data is turned on, you may adjust the following settings by going to Settings > Cellular > Cellular Data Options:

- To lessen your mobile data use, activate Low Data Mode by tapping Data Mode and then selecting Low Data Mode. When an iPhone is not connected to a Wi-Fi network, this mode prevents any further updates or background processes from occurring.
- If you are outside of your carrier's service area and would want to access the internet, you may activate or deactivate data roaming. Data

Roaming may be disabled when abroad to avoid incurring unnecessary fees.

The following features may be accessible on your iPhone (depending on its model, carrier, and location):

- Change the Voice Roaming setting: (CDMA). Disabling Voice Roaming will stop you from utilizing other carriers' networks and incurring additional fees. When your carrier's network isn't accessible, the iPhone won't have cellular (data or voice) service.
- Internet data may load more quickly when using 4G or LTE, but battery life may suffer as a result. Turning off 4G/LTE and choosing Voice & Data (VoLTE) or Data Only may be available.
- To extend your device's battery life, turn on Smart Data mode. Select 5G Auto by going to Voice & Data. In this option, your iPhone will switch to LTE automatically if 5G speeds don't significantly improve performance.
- FaceTime in high definition and better resolution is possible over 5G networks. Choose Data Mode, and then choose the option to Use More 5G Data.

Using Your iPhone As A Mobile Hotspot

To begin using your iPhone as a mobile hotspot, you must first activate the feature.

1. To activate Cellular Data, go to Settings > Cellular.
2. Select Personal Hotspot Setup, and then proceed as outlined in Allow others to use your iPhone to access the internet.

Limit the amount of data that applications and services may consume on the go

To enable or disable cellular data use, go to Settings > Cellular and then tap the toggle next to the app or service that needs it, such as Maps or Wi-Fi Assist.

When a switch is off, the iPhone will only utilize Wi-Fi for that function.

To clarify, Wi-Fi Assist is turned on by default. Wi-Fi Assist is a feature that uses cellular data to improve Wi-Fi connections when the former becomes unreliable. If you continue using your cellular data connection to access the web despite a spotty Wi-Fi signal, you may go over your monthly data limit and be charged extra.

SIM Card Lock

If your device utilizes a SIM card for phone calls or cellular data, you may lock the card using a personal identification number (PIN) to prevent others from using the card. After that, your card will automatically lock and prompt you for your PIN whenever you restart your device or remove the SIM card.

Adjust Your Settings For A Trip

Make sure your iPhone's settings are under those of the airline you're flying with. Some airlines allow you to leave your iPhone powered on if you go to airplane mode. Airplane mode automatically turns off Wi-Fi and Bluetooth®, so you can't make calls but can still play music, play games, view movies, and use other applications as usual.

Activate Aircraft Mode

To activate aircraft mode, launch the Control Center and choose the aircraft Mode Switch from the menu that appears.

Tap to turn on
airplane mode.

Airplane mode may be activated by touching the top left button on the Control Center screen.

Airplane mode may be toggled on and off in the same Settings menu. The status bar's Airplane Mode symbol changes to reflect whether or not airplane mode is active.

When in "airplane mode," activate Wi-Fi and Bluetooth.

You may use Wi-Fi and Bluetooth while flying if your airline permits it.

1. Launch the Control Center and activate the aircraft setting.
2. To activate Wi-Fi or Bluetooth, just tap the corresponding switches.

Tap to turn on Bluetooth.

Tap to turn on Wi-Fi.

Airplane mode in the settings panel indicates that Bluetooth and Wi-Fi have been disabled. Wi-Fi and Bluetooth toggles may be found in the top left corner of the Control Center.

Airplane mode may leave Wi-Fi and Bluetooth on if you switch them on while it's active. In the Settings menu, you may disable it once more.

Tap to turn off Bluetooth in airplane mode.

Tap to turn off Wi-Fi in airplane mode.

The iPhone Control Center. The Airplane mode button, Wi-Fi button, and Bluetooth button may all be found in the upper left corner of the device. We've activated the airplane mode, Bluetooth, and Wi-Fi. When using Airplane Mode, you may disable Bluetooth by tapping the Bluetooth button. Select Airplane Mode by tapping the Wi-Fi button.

Chapter Four

Start iPhone And Configure It

Activating and setting up your new iPhone requires access to the internet. Connecting your iPhone to a personal computer is another option for initial setup. If you have another iPhone, an iPad, or an Android device, you may move your data to your new iPhone.

If your iPhone is administered by your employer or other institution, you should consult an administrator before beginning setup.

Get Everything Ready To Go

Have the following on hand for a quick and easy setup:

- Wi-Fi network access (you may need the network's name and password) or cellular data connectivity (optional for iPhone 14 and later versions).
- Your Apple ID and password; you may create an Apple ID in the setup process if you don't already have one.
- When setting up Apple Pay, the details of any credit or debit cards you want to use.

If you buy an iPhone and immediately realize that you don't have enough capacity to make a full backup, don't worry; iCloud will provide you with as much space as you need for three weeks at no cost. To do a factory reset on your old smartphone, go to Settings > General > Factory Data Reset. Select the Get Started button and proceed with the on-screen prompts.

Awaken And Configure Your iPhone

1. The Apple logo will display if you press and hold the side button for a few seconds.

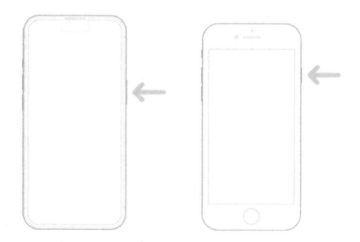

The right-side iPhone button is highlighted in green.

If your iPhone won't power on, try charging the battery first.

A quick way to activate VoiceOver, the iPhone's screen reader, for the visually impaired is to triple-click the side button (on an iPhone with Face ID) or the Home button (on older iPhone models). You may activate Zoom by double-tapping the screen with three fingers.

2. Pick one of the options below:

- To speed up the setup process, utilize Quick Start if you already own an iPhone or iPad running iOS 11 or iPadOS 13. To safely duplicate your settings, preferences, and iCloud Keychain across your devices, just place them close together and follow the on-screen instructions. After that, you may use your iCloud backup to bring over the remainder of your information and media to your new iPhone.

  You may also perform a wireless transfer of all your data across devices running iOS 12.4, iPadOS 13, or later. Until the migration is finished, keep all of your gadgets close to one another and connected.

  A cable connection between your gadgets is another option for data transmission.

- If you don't have access to a second device, choose Set Up Manually and proceed with the on-screen instructions.

Swap up your Android phone for an Apple iPhone.

When setting up a new iPhone, users with Android devices may import their data using the Move to iOS app.

If you have already finished setup and then decide you want to utilize Move to iOS, you will need to either delete your iPhone start anew, or manually transfer your data.

1. If you're using Android 4.0 or later, you can read up on how to make the transition to an iOS smartphone over at the Apple Support site.
2. Here's what you should do on your iPhone:
   - Observe the on-screen instructions.
   - Choose From Android on Transfer Your Apps & Data.
3. Follow these steps on your Android device:
   - Put your Wi-Fi on.
   - Initiate the iOS app called "Move."
   - Just do what it says on the screen.

Activate iPhone And Wake It Up

When you're not using your iPhone, it automatically locks for safety, goes to sleep to save power, and turns off the display. The iPhone can be instantly woken up and unlocked for usage again.

Awaken iPhone

The iPhone may be roused in one of two ways:

- A side button must be pressed.

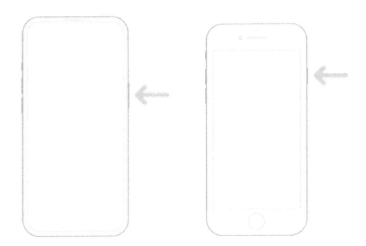

The right-side iPhone button is highlighted in green.

- Keep iPhone aloft.

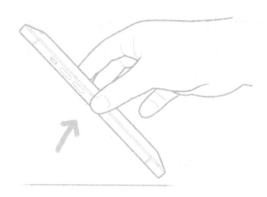

A hand picking up an iPhone from a desk.

Go to Settings > Display & Brightness to disable Raise to Wake.

- Select items by tapping them (iPhone SE only).

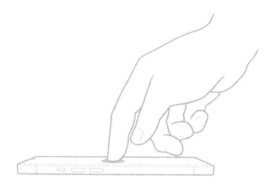

The iPhone may be woken with a touch of the screen.

Face ID iPhone Unlocking

1. To check your iPhone, you may either tap the screen to wake it up or lift it over your head.

2. As soon as you unlock your iPhone, the lock symbol animates open.
3. Drag your finger up from the bottom of the screen.

To lock the iPhone again, tap the side button. If you don't use your iPhone for a minute or more, it locks itself. If you have Attention Aware Features in Settings > Face ID & Passcode, however, your iPhone won't automatically lock or darken when it senses you're looking at it.

Use Touch Id To Unlock Your iPhone
You can get into your iPhone by pressing the Home button while using the finger you set up for Touch ID.

The bottom of the iPhone has the Home button (Touch ID).

To lock the iPhone again, tap the side button. If you don't use your iPhone for a minute or more, it locks itself.

Enter The Passcode To Unlock The iPhone

1. To unlock your iPhone with Face ID, swipe up from the bottom of the Lock Screen, or hit the Home button.
2. Type in the security code.

To lock the iPhone again, tap the side button. If you don't use your iPhone for a minute or more, it locks itself.

Get Your iPhone Ready For Cellular Service

A SIM card or electronic SIM is required for use with a cellular network on an iPhone. (Not all choices are available on all models or in all countries and areas. Obtain a SIM card and activate the service by contacting your service provider.

Make An Esim Work

Your carrier will issue you with an eSIM, which may be stored digitally on a compatible iPhone model. Turn on your iPhone and follow the on-screen steps to activate your eSIM via Carrier Activation or eSIM Quick Transfer, if supported by your carrier.

Once installation is complete, you may proceed to any of the following steps:

- Some carriers will be able to activate an eSIM for your iPhone without you having to do anything more than contact them. A "Finish Setting Up Cellular" alert will appear; touch it when it appears. You may also add an eSIM by going to Settings > Cellular and then tapping Set Up Cellular.

- Some carriers allow you to transfer your phone number from your old iPhone to your new iPhone without having to get in touch with them (needs iOS 16 or later on both devices) via a feature called eSIM Quick Transfer.

  On your new iPhone, go to Settings > Cellular, touch Set Up Cellular or Add eSIM, then press Transfer From Nearby iPhone or pick a phone number. You'll need to verify the transfer on your old iPhone by following the on-screen prompts.

  After you move your number to a new iPhone, it will no longer function on your old iPhone.

- Check out a QR Code issued by your service provider: Go to Settings > Cellular, then Set Up Cellular or Add eSIM, then press Use QR Code. (Other Options may need to be selected first.) Get your iPhone in the right spot to scan the code, or type in the information manually. Your carrier may supply you with a confirmation code that you'll need to use.

- If you want to port your number from a smartphone that isn't an iPhone, you'll need to get in touch with your old carrier.
- To begin service, download the mobile application of a supported provider: Activate your cellular service by downloading the carrier's app from the App Store.

If requested, connect your iPhone to an accessible Wi-Fi or cellular network. To activate an eSIM, you must have access to the internet.

Put In A Real SIM Card

A nano-SIM card may be purchased from a carrier or transferred from an older iPhone.

In the United States, iPhone models 14 and later cannot use a physical SIM card.

1. Press a paper clip or SIM eject tool into the SIM tray's tiny hole and press toward the iPhone to expel.

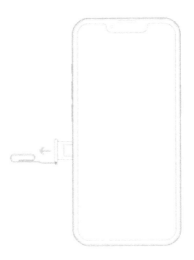

To eject and remove the tray on the left side of the iPhone, a paper clip or SIM eject tool must be put into the little hole.

The SIM tray may look different depending on the iPhone model and the nation or area you are in.

2. Take out the iPhone's tray.
3. Insert the SIM card into the slot. The right alignment is shown by the slanted corner.

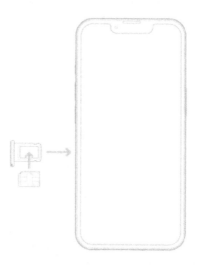

An iPhone with a SIM card is placed into its tray, the angled corner of which is seen at the top left.

4. Reinstall the iPhone's tray
5. If you already set up a PIN on the SIM, carefully enter the PIN when required.

Never, ever guess a SIM PIN. If you enter an erroneous SIM PIN three times in a row, your SIM will be permanently locked and you will be unable to use your phone or the internet via your carrier until you purchase a new SIM.

SIM card to electronic SIM card conversion
Any iPhone model that is compatible with your carrier's eSIM service will allow you to switch from a physical SIM to an eSIM.

1. Select the SIM card number by going to Settings > Cellular and tapping Set Up Cellular or Add eSIM.
2. Follow the on-screen prompts after tapping Convert to eSIM.

Cellular capabilities may not always be accessible, depending on factors such as your iPhone's model, your wireless provider, and your geographic location.

When planning your cellular strategy, be sure to include any necessary adjustments for data, voice, and roaming expenses, particularly if you intend to use your iPhone abroad.

For a price, several service providers unlock iPhones so that their customers may use them with other service providers. Contact your carrier for permission and setup details.

Get A Dual SIM iPhone

Double your iPhone's phone number capability with Dual SIM.

Some of the various applications of Dual SIM are as follows:

- Make professional and personal calls on separate numbers.

- When you go internationally, be sure to activate a local data plan.
- Keep your data and phone plans separate.

Your iPhone must be unlocked if you plan on using it with more than one carrier.

To activate Dual SIM, you will need:

- Dual-SIM capability (one physical SIM and one eSIM) is a feature of the iPhone XR, XS, 11, 12, 13, and subsequent (bought outside the US) models.
- Dual eSIM support for the iPhone 13/3GS/3GS Plus and subsequent models.

eSIM is not supported in all countries and areas.

Configure Dual SIM

1. Make sure you have two active lines by accessing Settings > Cellular and checking underneath SIMs.
2. Dual line activation is achieved by tapping a line followed by turning on this Line.
   You may also alter options such as Cellular Plan Label, Wi-Fi Calling (if available from your carrier), Calls on Other Devices, or SIM PIN. The icon may be seen in the phone's messaging and contact apps.

3. Choose the default line for cellular data—touch Cellular Data, then press a line. If you choose to Allow Cellular Data Switching, you may utilize either line based on coverage and signal strength.

If you have Data Roaming enabled and you go outside of your carrier's coverage area, you may pay additional fees.

4. Tap Default Voice Line, then choose a line to use as the default for voice calls.

Keep in mind the following while using Dual SIM:

• One of your lines must have Wi-Fi Calling activated for it to ring while the other is in use. To answer a call on one line while making a call on the other, if no Wi-Fi is available, the iPhone will utilize the cellular data plan of the line making the call. Charges may apply. To accept a call on another line, the line currently in use must be configured as the default line or have Allow Cellular Data Switching enabled (if it is not the default line).

• Any incoming calls (including those from emergency services) on the line that aren't enabled for Wi-Fi Calling will be sent to voicemail (if your carrier offers this feature) while you're using the other line, and you won't be notified that you missed a call.

If your carrier offers it, you may prevent calls from going to voicemail by setting up conditional call forwarding, which redirects calls from a busy or out-of-service line to another number.

- When you place a call on another device (such as a Mac) and have it routed via your Dual SIM iPhone, the call will go through your primary voice line.
- It is not possible to transfer an ongoing SMS/MMS message discussion from one line to another; instead, you must terminate the conversation and begin it over using the other line. If you use a line that isn't designated for cellular data to send an SMS/MMS attachment, you may be subject to extra fees.
- The cellular data connection is used for both Instant Hotspot and Personal Hotspot.

Get Your iPhone Online

Use a wireless network or your phone's data plan to go online with your iPhone.

Join Your iPhone To The Internet Wirelessly
1. To activate Wi-Fi, go to the menu and choose it.
2. Choose an option below:

- The network password, if prompted.
- Other: Enter the network's name, security type, and password to join a private network.

If the Wi-Fi symbol displays in the upper right of your screen, your iPhone is communicating with a wireless network. (Just load a website with Safari and see for yourself.) If you return to the same spot, your iPhone will automatically reconnect.

Participate In A Mobile Hotspot

Access the internet via cellular data via an existing Personal Hotspot created by another iPhone or iPad (Wi-Fi + Cellular).

1. Select the Personal Hotspot-sharing device by name in Settings > Wi-Fi.
2. If you're using an iOS device to share a Personal Hotspot and are prompted for a password, enter the one found in Settings > Cellular > Personal Hotspot.

Establish a cellular connection on your iPhone

If a Wi-Fi connection isn't available, the iPhone will use the cellular data network provided by your service provider. If your iPhone still won't sync, try these things:

1. Make sure your SIM card is both active and unlocked.
2. Go to Settings > Cellular.
3. Make sure that your cell data is enabled. Tap Cellular Data if you're using Dual SIM, then double-check the active connection. (Only one line may be used for mobile data.)

When an internet connection is required, the iPhone follows these steps in succession until it is established:

- Determines the most recently utilized accessible Wi-Fi network and attempts to connect to it.
- Displays available wireless networks and allows you to join one of them.
- Joins the mobile data network provided by your service provider

  If your iPhone is 5G compatible, it may switch to using cellular data rather than Wi-Fi when available. If so, the words Using 5G Cellular For Internet will appear underneath the name of the Wi-Fi network. Click the "Info" button next to the desired network's name, then choose "Use Wi-Fi for Internet" to revert to Wi-Fi.

If you can't access the internet via Wi-Fi, certain applications and services may have to use your cellular data plan, which might incur extra costs. To learn more about your mobile data plan's pricing, please contact your service provider.

Create An Email And Calendar Account

Create an iPhone email, contact, and calendar account.

In addition to iCloud and the native applications, the iPhone is compatible with Microsoft Exchange and other leading web-based email, contact, and calendar services. You may sign up for these services by creating an account.

Create An Email Address

1. Choose Accounts > Add Account > Mail > Settings.
2. Pick one of the options below:
   - Select a service, like as iCloud or Microsoft Exchange, and sign in with your credentials.
   - Select "Other," "Add Mail Account," and then input your login details.

Make A Contact List Today

1. Navigate to Accounts in Settings, then add an account under Contacts.
2. Pick one of the options below:

- Select a service, like as iCloud or Microsoft Exchange, and sign in with your credentials.
- If your company uses LDAP or CardDAV, choose "Other," then "Add LDAP Account" or "Add CardDAV Account," and finally input your server and account details.

Create An Online Calendar

1. Choose Calendar > Accounts > Add Account in Settings.
2. Pick one of the options below:
   - Pick a provider: Select a service, like as iCloud or Microsoft Exchange, and sign in with your credentials.
   - To add a CalDAV account, choose Other > Add CalDAV Account > Server Address > Username > Password.
   - Download iCalendar (.ics) feeds: To subscribe to an. ICS file, choose Other, then Add Subscribed Calendar. Alternatively, you may import an. ICS file from Mail.

If you enable iCloud Keychain on your iPhone, all of your other iOS devices will automatically sync to the most recent version of your account information.

Put The iPhone On Charge

The lithium-ion rechargeable battery used inside the iPhone offers the highest possible performance levels. Lithium-ion batteries feature a better power density, a longer lifespan, a lower self-discharge rate, and less environmental impact than their conventional counterparts.

How To Get The Battery Charged

The charging status of the battery is shown by a lightning bolt symbol.

The battery symbol in the top-right corner indicates the battery level or charging status. It may take longer to charge your iPhone while you're syncing or using it.

If your iPhone's battery is critically low, you may see an almost empty battery icon, suggesting that you must plug it in for at least 10 minutes before using it again. If your iPhone's battery is critically low when you plug it in to charge, you may have to wait up to two minutes for the low battery picture to show on the screen.

Battery charging, please.

The iPhone may be charged in a variety of ways.

- Use the provided charging cable in conjunction with an Apple USB power adapter or compatible power adapter (available separately) to charge your iPhone.

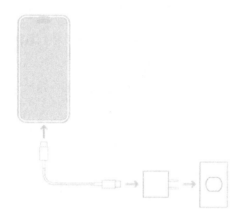

Apple iPhone with its charging cable inserted into a wall socket.

- To charge your iPhone wirelessly, set it face down on a Qi-certified charger or a MagSafe charger (attached to an Apple 20W USB-C power adapter or other compatible power converter). (The MagSafe and MagSafe Duo Chargers, as well as AC wall adapters and Qi-compatible chargers, are available as accessories.).

Also, Qi-certified chargers and power adapters from third parties that meet local, national, and international safety laws may be used.

- Wire iPhone to PC.

  When connecting an iPhone to a computer, be sure the computer is switched on; otherwise, the iPhone's battery may drain instead of charge. To verify that your iPhone is charging, tap the battery symbol.

  A high-power USB port on your keyboard is required if you want to use your keyboard to charge your iPhone.

When you plug your iPhone into a wall charger or set it on a wireless charger, iCloud backups, and wireless PC syncs may begin automatically.

Do not insert the charging cable into the iPhone's port if there is any doubt that the port is dry.

Boost iPhone Charger Performance

Your iPhone's battery may last longer thanks to a feature that limits the amount of time it spends in the fully charged state. Using machine learning, this option anticipates when you'll need your device and stops charging at 80% till then.

1. Select Battery > Battery Health & Charging from the Settings menu.
2. Pick one of the options below:
   - On iPhone 14 and previous models: Turn on Optimized Battery Charging.
   - Select Optimized Battery Charging from the Charging Optimization menu for iPhone 15 models.

Use and configuration factors into battery life and recharge cycles.

Apple or an Apple Authorized Service Provider is the only company authorized to service or recycle iPhone batteries.

Chapter Five

Modify The Ringtone And Vibrations

The ringtone, vibrate, and alert noises that play on your iPhone may all be customized under the Settings menu.

When you execute certain activities, such as touching and holding any icon on the Home Screen, a compatible model will provide haptic feedback in the form of a vibration.

Modify The Volume And Vibration Settings

1. Select "Sounds & Haptics" under "Settings."
2. The slider underneath Ringtone and Alert Volume controls the overall volume.
3. To configure the tones and vibration patterns for sounds, choose a sound type, such as ringtone or text tone.
4. Just choose one of the following:
   - Select a mood from the dropdown.
     Text tones are used as notifications for things like fresh voicemail and text messages, whereas ringtones are used for incoming calls, clock alarms, and the clock timer.

- Select a vibration pattern from the list that appears when you hit Vibration, or tap Create New Vibration to make your own.

You may customize the iPhone's ringtones, alerts, and other sounds for individual users. To set a ringtone and text tone for a contact, open Contacts, press the contact's name, and then hit Edit.

Flip The Switch For Tactile Feedback

1. Select Sounds & Haptics under Settings on compatible devices.
2. System Haptics may be toggled on and off.

   If you turn off System Haptics, you won't be notified of incoming calls or alarms via vibrations.

When switched on or off, iPhones 14 and later may play a custom sound.

1. Navigate to Audio/Video > Settings > Accessibility.
2. Play the Sounds of Power On and Off.

The Do Not Disturb setting should be checked in the Control Center if you aren't getting calls or notifications when you should be. If the Do Not Disturb icon is in the foreground, tapping it will disable the feature.

Make Use Of The Action Button

Make use of the Action button and set your preferences on the iPhone 15 Pro and iPhone 15 Pro Max.

An iPhone 15 Pro and iPhone 15 Pro Max contain an Action button instead of the Ring/Silent option. When you hit the Action button, you may customize what happens. The button is convenient for frequent tasks since it is easily accessible. (The position of the button labeled "Action" is seen below.) It's simple to modify the action when you decide you want to utilize it for a new purpose.

Image demonstrating the position of the Action button on the left side of the iPhone 15 Pro. In Preferences, click the Action Button to modify the button's behavior.

Personalize The Action Button

iPhone 15 Pro and iPhone 15 Pro Max now allow users to personalize their Action button.

1. Choose Action Button > Settings.

You'll see the iPhone's side with icons that stand in for the many functions you may choose for the Action button.

The Action button configuration window. The Camera option was selected. The camera's right and left sides also house other controls, such as Silent Mode and the Flashlight. You may switch between activities by tapping the dots that appear under them. Below the chosen action, Camera is a

menu of Camera choices you may touch to assign to the Action button.

2. Swipe to the desired action; its name will show below the dots.

   You may silence your iPhone 15 Pro or 15 Pro Max with a swipe to the Bell Slash button in the Actions section of the Control Center. Swipe to the next option to change your mind.

3. You may check what other choices you have for the current activity by tapping the Menu button that displays if necessary.

   For the Shortcuts and Accessibility actions to take effect, you must first press the blue button that appears underneath the action and then choose an option.

Icon	Action
	*Silent mode:* Turn Silent mode on or off.
	Focus: Turn a specific Focus on or off.
	Camera: Open the Camera app to quickly take a photo, selfie, video, portrait, or portrait selfie.
	Flashlight: Turn the flashlight on or off.
	Voice Memo: Start or stop recording a voice memo.
	Magnifier: Open the Magnifier app.

Shortcut: Open an app or run your favorite shortcut.

 Accessibility: Quickly access your favorite accessibility feature.

No
Action   Do nothing.

The Button Labeled "Action"

Holding down the Action button causes it to carry out its designated action.

The Action button may be used to activate or deactivate several features. If you want to set your iPhone into Silent Mode, for instance, you may do it by pressing and holding the Action button. Silent mode may be disabled by pressing and holding the Action button once more.

Customize Your Lock Screen With Background

You may customize your Lock Screen by picking a background, presenting a favorite picture, altering the typeface of the time, adding widgets, and more.

Add Lock Screens, switch between them, and connect them to Focuses. You may, for instance, customize a work-related Lock Screen.

Make A Custom Lock Screen

1. To access the Customize option and the Add New button, touch and hold the Lock Screen.
   If you don't see them, press and hold the Lock Screen once again, and then enter your PIN.
2. To make changes to an existing Lock Screen, slide to the desired screen, choose Customize, and then select Lock Screen. Alternatively, you may press the Add New option to create a new Lock Screen.

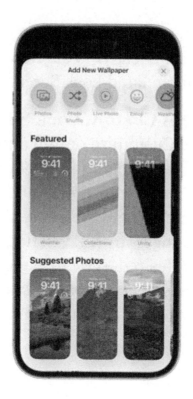

On the Add New Wallpaper page, you may choose from a wide variety of categories, including Featured and Suggested Photos, to choose the perfect background for your iPhone's Lock page. There are options to customize the Lock Screen with images, contacts, a random photo feature, emoticons, and the current weather at the top of the screen.

3. If you're making a new Lock Screen, touch one of the wallpaper selections to pick it as your Lock Screen.

4. You may alter the size, color, and style of the clock by tapping it.

   For solid typefaces, you may adjust the weight by using the slider.

5. Widgets that display information like the day's headlines, the weather, and upcoming events may be added by selecting Add Widgets, the current date, or the field just below the clock.

Currently being tweaked: a personalized Lock Screen. The date, the time, and a button to add widgets are all elements that may be personalized.

6. Press Add or Done, then press Set as Wallpaper Pair or Customize Home Screen.
   - You may decide whether the wallpaper will be used on the Home Screen as well as the Lock Screen. Tap Set as Wallpaper Pair.
   - Alter the Home Screen in other ways: Select the Home screen settings to modify. To alter the wallpaper, just touch the desired hue, or utilize the Photo On Rectangle or Blur buttons, respectively.

Set A Picture To Lock Your Screen

The picture you choose for your Lock Screen gives you a lot of flexibility in terms of placement, style, and more.

Just choose one of the following:

- To relocate a chosen picture, pinch open to zoom in, drag with two fingers to the new location, then pinch closed to zoom out.
- Modify the look of the pictures: To experiment with alternative picture effects using complimentary color filters and typography, just swipe left or right.
- If your shot has many subjects (such as people, dogs, or the sky), you may create a layered effect

by tapping the More button in the lower right corner and then selecting Depth Effect.

Models that may use the multilayered effect already exist. Layering may not be possible if the topic is too high or too low, or if it obscures too much of the clock.

- Use a Live Photo to create a motion effect by tapping the Play button in the bottom left of the screen when the device wakes up. This will play the Live Photo in slow motion.
- Photo Shuffle's frequency may be adjusted by hitting the More button and then choosing an option under Shuffle Frequency after seeing a sample of the photographs in the gallery using the Browse button.

Tip: Alternatively, you may upload a picture straight from your photo library to your Home Screen and Lock Screen. Select a picture from your library in the Photos app, and then hit the share button. Select Use as Wallpaper from the drop-down menu, hit Add, and then decide whether you want to use it as your home screen wallpaper or lock screen wallpaper.

Create A Lock Screen Concentrate

Focus allows you to work more efficiently by blocking out irrelevant stimuli. Focuses may be configured to temporarily disable all notifications or to enable just selected notifications (such as those relevant to your current activity). When you associate a Focus with a Lock Screen, the settings for that Focus will take effect anytime you utilize that Lock Screen.

1. To access the customization options, touch and hold the Lock Screen until the button appears at the bottom.
2. Focus choices, such as Do Not Disturb, Personal, Sleep, and Work, may be accessed by tapping the Focus icon in the wallpaper's lower-right corner.

   If you don't see Focus in the wallpaper's lower-right corner, you need to adjust your Focus settings.

3. Choose a Focus, and then click the X to dismiss it.

Adjust The Settings For Your Lock Screen

A personalized Lock Screen may be updated after it has been first created.

1. To access the Customize option and the Add New button, touch and hold the Lock Screen.
   If you don't see them, press and hold the Lock Screen once again, and then enter your PIN.
2. A new screen will appear; swipe to it, press Customize, and then tap Lock Screen.
3. You may alter the size, color, and style of the clock by tapping it.
4. Widgets that display information like the day's headlines, the weather, and upcoming events may be added by selecting Add Widgets, the current date, or the field just below the clock.
5. Press Add or Done, then press Set as Wallpaper Pair or Customize Home Screen.

Change The Secure Screen

Throughout the day, you may swap between many different personalized Lock Screens that you've created.

1. To access the customization options, touch and hold the Lock Screen until the button appears at the bottom.
2. Swipe to the Lock Screen you wish to use, then press it.

When you go from one Lock Screen to another, if the previous Lock Screen was linked to a different Focus, the Focus will likewise change.

Remove a Passcode Lock

Lock Screens that are no longer necessary may be removed.

1. To access the customization options, touch and hold the Lock Screen until the button appears at the bottom.
2. To remove a Lock Screen, swipe to it, slide up, then hit the Trash icon and finally the Delete This Wallpaper option.

Your iPhone Background May Be Changed

Both the Lock Screen and the Home Screen wallpaper may be customized on an iPhone. You have the option of selecting a new background either from the Settings menu or the Lock Screen's wallpaper collection.

This is the Wallpaper Settings page, where you may alter the current wallpaper for the Home page and Lock Screen, as well as add new wallpapers.

Add New Wallpaper

1. To add new wallpaper, go to Wallpaper Settings. The background gallery loads.
2. Just choose one of the following:
   - Tap a button at the top of the wallpaper gallery—for example, Photos, Photo Shuffle, Live Photo, and so on—to build your

wallpaper with a photo, an emoji pattern, an image of your local weather, and more.

- The featured wallpaper collections (Collections, Astronomy, Weather, etc.) are at your disposal.

3. Select "Add," then pick an action from the list:
   - You have the option of using this wallpaper as both your Lock Screen and Home Screen background. Tap Set as Wallpaper Pair.
   - Alter the Home Screen in other ways: Select the Home screen settings to modify. To alter the wallpaper, just touch the desired hue, or utilize the Photo On Rectangle or Blur buttons, respectively.

Utilize Standby On Your iPhone
StandBy allows you to watch content from a distance while your iPhone is recharging.

StandBy allows you to transform your iPhone into a variety of useful devices, like a bedside clock, a picture frame, a display for displaying widgets or Live Activities on full screen, and more.

The digital time is shown on the screen of a charging iPhone in StandBy, which is resting on its side.

Put On The Standby

1. Make sure StandBy is on by navigating to Settings > StandBy.
2. Put the iPhone on its side while it is charging, and leave it there.
3. A side button must be pressed.
4. To navigate between widgets, images, and clocks, swipe either left or right. To toggle between the several available perspectives, just swipe up or down.

If you choose Night Mode for StandBy, the screen will automatically adjust to the low light levels of the night and show objects with a red tinge, making them less distracting while you sleep.

In dim lighting, the Clock and Calendar widgets on an iPhone in Standby mode appear red.

With the Always-On display (on iPhone 14 Pro, iPhone 14 Pro Max, iPhone 15 Pro, and iPhone 15 Pro Max), StandBy remains on to offer vital information. StandBy may be activated instantly on any other iPhone by touching the screen, bumping the table your iPhone is sitting on, or using Siri.

StandBy remembers your preferred view, whether it is a clock, photographs, or widgets, at each place where you charge your iPhone using MagSafe. You may put up pictures of the family in the kitchen and set an alarm on it in the bedroom.

Categorize Your Applications

Create folders on your iPhone to categorize your applications.

You may create folders for your applications to make them more manageable on the Home Screen pages.

Make Folders

1. Touch and hold the Home Screen backdrop until the applications begin to jitter.
2. Drag one app atop another app to create a folder.
3. Simply drop new programs inside the container. The application folder might contain many pages.
4. Touch and hold the folder you want to rename, choose Rename, and then type in the new name. If the applications begin to bounce, touch the Home Screen wallpaper and try again.
5. When you're done, choose Done, and then double-tap the Home Screen wallpaper.

Select the folder you want to remove by tapping on it, then dragging all the applications out of it. The folder will be removed immediately.

The App Library retains its structure regardless of how you arrange your applications on the Home Screen.

How To Promote An App To The Main Screen

How to Promote an App to the Main Screen from a Subfolder

To make an app more accessible, you may transfer it from its current location in a folder to the Home Screen.

1. Navigate to the app's folder on the Home Screen, hit the folder's icon, and launch the app.
2. Simply tap and hold the app until it starts to wiggle.
3. Copy and paste the app's icon from the folder onto the Home Screen.

Adjust, And Delete Widgets On The iPhone

Add, modify, and delete widgets on iPhone Weather, Reminders, and Home widgets on the iPhone Home Screen. Both the Reminders and Home widgets have clickable elements.

What do you mean by the term "widgets"?

Widgets allow you to see timely data such as today's news, the weather, upcoming events, and remaining battery life. You may see widgets in Today see and add them to your Home Screen or Lock Screen to keep this information at your fingertips.

Widgets for Music, Podcasts, Safari, Home, Contacts, and more can all be accessed directly from the Home Screen or Lock Screen, negating the need to launch the corresponding app. If you're using a music or podcast widget, for instance, you may start playing an item by tapping the Play button.

Install A New Widget On Your Desktop

1. Touch and hold the Home Screen background until the applications start to wiggle, and then drag the widget to the page of the Home Screen where you want it to appear.
2. Select the Add Widget menu item to access the widget library.
3. Find the widget you need by scrolling or searching, tapping it, and then swiping between the available sizes.
   Size-specific information is shown.
4. When the appropriate size is shown, choose Add Widget.
5. While the applications are still bouncing, drag the widget to its new location and press Done.

Widgets may also be placed on the Lock Screen.

A Smart Stack (shown by the dots) is a collection of widgets that respond to factors like the time of day, your current location, and the actions you've taken to provide you with the most pertinent widget at the most relevant moment. Widgets in a Smart Stack may be seen by adding it to the Home Screen and then swiping up and down through it.

Use The Available Widgets

You may conduct actions by touching widgets on your Home Screen or Lock Screen. Without switching apps, you can just touch an item to mark it as complete in the To-Do list widget, start a podcast episode in the Podcasts widget, or switch on the living room lights in the Home widget.

Replace a Home Screen widget with a new one

Most widgets allow you to alter their appearance and the data they show directly from your Home Screen. For a Mail widget, for instance, tapping the mailbox shown in the widget and selecting a different mailbox causes the messages in the selected mailbox to be presented in the widget. Alternately, you may program a Smart Stack to cycle between its widgets depending on factors such as your current location, the time of day, and the tasks you've just completed.

1. Touching and holding a widget on the Home Screen will bring up a menu of shortcuts.
2. Select the widget's settings by selecting the Edit button (or the Edit Stack button in the case of a Smart Stack).

   The widgets in a Smart Stack may be rearranged by dragging them up and down inside the stack, moved to the Home Screen, or deleted by hitting the minus symbol (-) in the top left corner of the widget.

   If you enable Widget Suggestions, your Smart Stack will populate with useful widgets for applications you use when you need them. The widget may be permanently added to your stack using the options menu.

3. Finished by tapping.

Touch and holding a widget on the Home Screen will bring up a selection of fast actions.

To delete a widget, select it, then hit the Remove button.

The Today View Widget Page
Swipe right from the left side of the Home Screen to get Today View, where you may browse up and down among various widgets.

Widgets showing in Today View, including the Reminders, Photos, Battery, Calendar, and Tips widgets and more.

Browse Today's widgets Access content even while your iPhone is locked

1. To enable Face ID or Touch ID and passcode on your iPhone, go to Settings > Face ID & Passcode or Settings > Touch ID & Passcode, respectively.
2. Type in the security code.
3. Turn enable Today View and Search (below Allow Access When Locked).

Home Screen App And Widget Replacement

iPhone's Home Screen app and widget placement may be changed.

The Home Screen is highly customizable, allowing you to rearrange widgets and applications, hide pages temporarily, direct program downloads to a specific location, and much more.

You may make a certain page of your Home Screen available during a specific Focus by putting all the applications and widgets you use for that Focus (say, your Work Focus) on that page.

Move Applications And Widgets Around

Move applications and widgets around on your iPhone Touch and hold any app or widget on the Home Screen, then tap Edit Home Screen.

1. There is a wiggle in the applications.
    Put an app where it belongs by dragging it there:
2. A different section of the same page
    *   An alternative Start Menu

The widget or application should be dragged to the right side of the display. It might take a moment for the new page to load. The number of open tabs and the currently active tab are shown by the dots above the Dock.

Apps on the Home Screen are being juggled about with an arrow indicating the movement of one app to the next page.

3. When you're done, either hit the Home button (if your iPhone has one) or touch the Done button (on older iPhones).

Bring Back The Factory Settings

Bring back the factory settings for the Home screen and all the applications.

1. Tap General > Erase All Content and Settings to wipe your iPhone.
2. To do this, go to Settings, then Home, and finally Reset.

Downloaded applications replace those that arrived with your iPhone and are wiped clean and rearranged alphabetically.

Eliminate Your iPhone Software

The iPhone makes it simple to eliminate software. You can always reinstall the applications in the future if you change your mind.

Remove An App From The Home Screen

Just choose one of the following:

- Remove an app from the Home Screen: Touch and hold the app on the Home Screen, touch Remove App, then tap Remove from Home Screen to retain it in App Library or hit erase App to erase it from the iPhone.
- Eliminate an app from your Home screen and App Library: After touching and holding the app in the App Library, choose Delete App.

You can always reinstall an app from the app store if you change your mind.

The following Apple applications that come preinstalled on your iPhone may be deleted in addition to any third-party apps:

- Books
- Calculator
- Calendar
- Clock
- Compass
- You can still access your contacts using the Phone app, as well as Messages, Mail, and FaceTime.
- FaceTime
- Files
- Remove this app to disable seeing locations in the Find My app on that device alone. This does not disable location sharing or Find My for your device or things.
- Fitness
- Freeform
- Health
- Home
- iTunes Market
- Magnifier
- Mail
- Maps

- Measure
- Music
- News
- Notes
- Podcasts
- Reminders
- Shortcuts
- Stocks
- Tips
- Translate
- TV
- Recollections in Verbal Form
- Wallet (Uninstalling this program won't clear up your iCloud card and pass data.)
- Watch
- Weather

When you uninstall an in-built app from your Home Screen, you also uninstall all associated data and settings. There may be unintended consequences if you delete a program from the system's default installation.

Chapter Six

Personalize The Control Center

The iPhone's Control Center provides quick access to frequently used settings and applications, including Airplane Mode, Do Not Disturb, Flashlight, Volume, and Brightness.

Throw Open The Controls

- A Face ID-enabled iPhone can: Use your right thumb to swipe down from the top. Swipe up from the bottom to dismiss the Control Center.
- If your iPhone has a Home button, swipe up from the bottom to access it. Swipe down or hit the Home button to exit the Control Center.

The Control Panel has additional options available.

There are a lot of customizable settings. Touch and holding a control will reveal the possible adjustments. In Control Center, you may do actions such as these, for instance:

- To access AirDrop settings, touch and hold the leftmost set of buttons, then press the icon.
- To take a picture, video, or "selfie," just touch and hold the camera button.

Touch and hold to
see Camera options.

The Airplane Mode, Cellular Data, Wi-Fi, and Bluetooth Settings are all located in the upper left corner of the Control Center on the left screen. The Camera button appears in the right-hand corner. View other shortcuts for the Camera, including "Take Selfie," "Record Video," "Take Portrait," and "Take Portrait Selfie," on the screen to the right.

Incorporate And Arrange Sliders

Many applications, including the Calculator, Notes, Voice Memos, and more, may have additional controls and shortcuts added to Control Center.

1. In Settings, choose Control Center.
2. To insert or delete a control, click the corresponding Insert or Delete button.
3. Drag and drop a control to a new location after touching the Reorder button that appears next to it.

Break your wireless connection temporarily

To turn Wi-Fi on or off, use the Control Center's Wi-Fi Switch button.

If you press and hold the Wi-Fi Switch button, you'll be able to read the name of the currently active Wi-Fi network.

AirPlay and AirDrop continue to function, and the iPhone automatically reconnects to previously joined networks when you move to a new area or restart the device. Go to "Settings" > "Wi-Fi" to disable it.

Put away your Bluetooth gadgets for the time being

To enable Bluetooth connections, hit the Bluetooth Switch button in the Control Center.

Disconnecting from devices doesn't disable Bluetooth®, so location services and other features may still be used. To disable Bluetooth, choose Bluetooth from the menu at the top of your screen and then select Off. Simply tapping the Bluetooth Switch button in the Control Center will re-enable Bluetooth.

Disable app access to the Control Center.

Go to Settings > Control Center, then switch off Access Within Apps.

Adjust The Screen's Orientation Or Secure It
When you turn your iPhone, you might see something new in several applications.

In the backdrop, the iPhone shows a Calendar screen, displaying one day's events in portrait mode; in the foreground, the iPhone is turned to landscape orientation, which displays the Calendar events for the complete week including the same day.

Screen rotation locks and unlocks

If you don't want your screen to rotate when you turn your iPhone, you can lock the orientation.

Launch the Settings menu and choose the Lock Orientation option.

The Lock Orientation icon in the status bar will display (on compatible devices) when the screen orientation is locked.

Check For Alerts And Take Action On Them

You may learn about new developments, such as missed calls or changed event dates, via notifications. You may personalize your notification settings so you see only what's essential to you.

If you haven't muted them with a Focus, your iPhone will show you alerts as they come in; they'll slide up from the bottom of the screen. Lock Screen displays them in many different ways, including a count view, a stacking view, and an extended list view. The Lock Screen's notification arrangement may be adjusted with a pinch of the screen.

While you're using an app, you could be asked how you want to get alerts from it—immediately, not at all, or in a scheduled summary. In the future, you may modify this under Preferences > Notifications.

The Notification Center is where you can find any new alerts.

You may access your alerts in the Notification Center by:

- Screen Lock: Swipe up from the center.
- Swipe down from the screen's upper-center on all other devices. Then, if there are any previous alerts, you may see them by scrolling up.

If you have an iPhone with a Home button, you may dismiss the Notification Center by swiping your finger up from the bottom of the screen.

React To Alerts

Notifications from different apps are sorted into several categories in the Notification Center and on the Lock Screen. Some applications may also have in-app organization options for grouping notifications, such as by thread or subject. Notices that are related to one another are stacked together, with the most current one on top.

Just choose one of the following:

- To see individual alerts inside a group: Promptly ring the bell. Simply choose Show Less from the menu to hide the collection.
- Hold the notice on your screen.
- To launch a notification app: Tap the notification.

Set Up A Briefing Summary

You may decrease the number of interruptions in your day by setting up a summary of your alerts to be sent at a time of your choosing.

Your current activity is used to automatically sort the notification summary, putting the most important alerts at the top. The summary is particularly helpful since it lets you deal with alerts whenever it's convenient for you. Focus takes this a step further by blocking distracting alerts while you're trying to concentrate on anything.

1. To activate Scheduled Summary, go to Settings > Notifications > Scheduled Summary.
2. Pick the programs that will be included in the summary.
3. Time yourself as you summarize. You may get yet another summary by selecting the Add Summary option.
4. Select the applications you wish to include in your summary by tapping the A to Z button that appears under applications in Summary.

Access, Manage, And Silence Alerts

Any of the following may be done in response to iPhone alerts:

- How to respond to a message that pops up in another app: It just takes a tap to open, and a swipe up to close.
- Clear notifications: Swipe left on a notice or collection of alerts, then hit Clear or Clear All.
- To temporarily silence app alerts, swipe left on the notification or group of alerts, choose Options, and then select the desired period using the clock. This takes them immediately to the Notification Center and prohibits them from displaying on the Lock Screen, playing a sound, lighting up the screen, or presenting a banner.
- Swipe the notification to the left in the Notification Center, choose Options, and then select Unmute to restore the notification's visibility and sound.
- Stop receiving alerts from a certain app or category of apps: To disable a notification or a set of notifications, swipe left on them, choose Options, and finally select Turn Off.
- Change how an app shows notifications: Swipe left on a notice, select Options, then press View Settings.
- Delete all alerts from the Notifications tray: To delete all notifications, open Notification Center and choose Clear.
- Active the Do Not Disturb mode.

You could be advised to disable alerts for an app if you haven't used it in a while.

Display Recent Alerts When Locked In

The Lock Screen is where you may enable Notification Center access.

1. To enable Face ID or Touch ID and passcode on your iPhone, go to Settings > Face ID & Passcode or Settings > Touch ID & Passcode, respectively.
2. Type in the security code.
3. After enabling Allow Access When Locked, scroll down and activate Notification Center.

Adjust Your iPhone's Alert Settings

Adjust the alarm volume; enable location-based alerts and messages from the government and more under Settings.

Modify Your Alert Preferences

Most notification settings may be adjusted for each app. You may customize the appearance of app alerts when the screen is unlocked, choose a sound to play when a notice is received, and more.

1. Choose Notifications > Settings.
2. Modify the Lock Screen notifications whatever you like:

- Just see how many alerts there are by clicking the Count button.
- Check out the different piles of alerts for each app: To stack, tap.
- Check out a rundown of all the alerts: Listen to the List.

Pinch the alerts on the Lock Screen to rearrange their placement.

3. Scheduled Summaries may be activated by selecting Scheduled Summary from the menu after a notice.
4. After selecting Always, When Unlocked, or Never from the Show Previews menu, you may toggle the previews on and off by tapping the Back button in the upper left.
Text (from Messages and Mail) and invitation information (from Calendar) are only two examples of what may be previewed. This preference may be overridden per-app.
5. To enable or disable notifications for a specific app, tap the app's Notification Style toggle switch.

Turn Time Sensitive alerts on or off depending on whether you want immediate or planned delivery of alerts after enabling Allow Notifications.

Many applications also allow you to customize the tone and badges that are shown in response to notifications.

6. Select Notification Grouping and then set the desired notification groupings:
   - The app's alerts are automatically categorized by the app's internal parameters, such as by thread or subject.
   - Notifications from the same app are categorized under the same tab.
   - Deactivate the ability to group.

To turn off alerts individually for applications, click on Settings > alerts > Siri Suggestions, then turn off any app.

The iPhone app Focus pauses notifications so you can work uninterrupted. A digest of your missed alerts may be sent to you at a time of your choosing. Please see Notification Summaries for Scheduling.

You may toggle location-based notifications on or off.

Some applications may give you location-specific notifications that are useful at the moment. When you reach a certain area, for instance, you may get a notification reminding you to make a phone call.

You may disable these notifications if you prefer not to receive them.

1. To enable Location Services, choose Privacy & Security > Settings.
2. Awaken the location services.
3. Select an app from the list, and then decide whether or not to allow location sharing for that app.

Access web app push notifications through the web

When you add a web app's website icon to your Home Screen, you'll be able to get normal Web Push alerts from the app. You may stay abreast of app happenings with the help of web push notifications. You may get alerts and badges inside the web app, identical to those you see on your iPhone, after you sign up for push notifications within the app.

Sign Up For Official Warnings

You may enable notifications from the Government Alerts list in certain locations. On an iPhone in the United States, for instance, you may opt-in or out of receiving National notifications, as well as AMBER,

Public Safety, and Emergency Alerts (which include both Severe and Extreme Imminent Threat notifications). The Japan Meteorological Agency has developed emergency earthquake alerts for the iPhone in Japan.

1. Choose Notifications > Settings.
2. To activate the notifications you need, just scroll down to the "Government Alerts" section.

The availability of government alerts and their effectiveness depend on the user's iPhone model and carrier.

Install An iPhone Focus

Focus is a function that helps you eliminate distractions and create limits. When you need to zero down on a certain task, you may either tweak one of the pre-set Focuses like "Work," "Personal," or "Sleep," or make your own. To let other people and applications know you're working, you may use Focus to temporarily quiet all notifications or to enable just certain alerts, such as those that pertain to your task.

When a Focus is associated with a particular Lock Screen, activating it is as easy as swiping to that Lock Screen.

Similarly, during a Focus you may make a certain page of your Home Screen that only contains applications connected to that Focus your primary screen. Home Screen pages containing applications and widgets pertinent to the Focus you're building up are also suggested by the iPhone.

Tip: To rapidly quiet all alerts, open Control Center, hit Focus, then switch on Do Not Disturb.

Focusing In On

1. Select a Focus from the list that appears once you select Settings > Focus, such as Do Not Disturb, Personal, Sleep, or Work.

   You do not need to configure all of the following steps for the Focus you have chosen.

The five available Focus settings (Do Not Disturb, No messages during calls, Sleep, Personal, and Work) are shown on the screen. Focus preferences may be shared across Apple devices when the Share Across Devices option is activated.

2. Choose which applications and contacts may interrupt your Focus with alerts.

   After you pick which persons and applications to enable notifications from, an Options link appears.

3. Choose an action from the following after tapping Options:
   - Toggle the Show On Lock Screen switch to display previously muted alerts or send them to the Notification Center.
   - To maintain focus, please activate the Dim Lock Screen.
   - The Home Screen app's notification badges may be hidden by activating Hide Notification Badges.
4. When you're done making selections, you may return to the previous screen by clicking the Back button.
5. Select a new Lock Screen to use with this Focus by tapping the preview of a different Lock Screen located under the Customize Screens section, and then tapping Done at the screen's top.
6. Touch the Home Screen preview located under Customize Screens, choose a Home Screen page, and then touch Done to apply your selection to this Focus.

   Apps and widgets specific to the Focus you're putting up will show up as possibilities on the Home Screen.

7. Tap the Back button, then enable Share Across Devices to have your Focus synced across all of your signed-in Apple devices.

Once you've set up your Focus, you can always go back to Settings > Focus to alter the previously selected settings.

Focuses may be turned on and off manually or on a predetermined timetable using the Control Center.

Set Up Sleep in Health allows you to modify your sleep routine by changing your next bedtime and wakeup time.

Use Filter In Focus

When you set up a Focus, you can apply app filters that define what information applications will display during the Focus. During the Focus, you have the option of switching between many email and calendar accounts.

1. To apply filters to a certain Focus, go to the app's settings and then press the desired Focus.
2. Select Add Filter under Focus Filters.
3. Select the data you'd want to utilize from a certain app by tapping on it and then on it again during the Focus:

- Select which calendars to display during the designated Focus time.
- Select which email accounts you'd want to check during the Focus.
- Messages: Select which discussions from your inbox you want to see during the Focus, for example, just those from persons you have permitted notifications from.
- Select the Tab Group you want to utilize in Safari when in Focus mode.

4. To apply this filter to the Focus, tap the Add button.

Make Your Custom Focus

You may make your own Custom Focus if you want to focus on anything outside the predefined alternatives.

A Focus setup page for one of the many available Focus modes, including Custom, Driving, Fitness, Gaming, Mindfulness, and Reading.

1. Navigate to Preferences > Focus.
2. Select Custom by clicking the Add button in the upper right.
3. To give your Focus a name, type it in and hit Return.
4. To designate your Focus, choose an appropriate color and icon, and then press Next.
5. Select "Customize Focus," and then adjust the available settings.

Focus preferences should be kept current across all of your Apple devices.

Focus preferences are synced across all devices when the same Apple ID is used.

You may activate Share Across Devices by going to Settings > Focus.

Focus filters are only saved locally on the device they are created for.

Focus On Alerts May Be Enabled Or Muted

When configuring a Focus, you may choose to disable or enable alerts from certain contacts and applications. Establish a Work Focus and restrict alerts to those from colleagues and work-related applications, for instance.

1. Select a Focus from the Settings menu (DND, Personal, Sleep, or Work, for example), and then save your changes.
2. Select Individuals (or Pick Individuals) and then either:
   - Permit selected individuals: touch Allow Notifications From, touch the Add People option, then pick from your contacts.

Allowing calls from certain caller groups and repeated calls (from the same caller twice or more within three minutes) are further possibilities.

- Keep some individuals quiet: Click the Silence Notifications From button, then the Add People button.

In addition, you have the option to enable calls from muted users.

You can always make exceptions for calls from your emergency contacts in Focus.

You may choose which applications' alerts you want to receive or ignore during a Focus

1. Select a Focus from the Settings menu (DND, Personal, Sleep, or Work, for example), and then save your changes.
2. Select Apps (or Select Apps) and then either:
   - Permit selected app usage: Select applications to get notifications from by tapping the Allow Notifications From button and then tapping the Add applications button.
   - Apps that can be muted: To disable alerts from certain applications, choose them after tapping the Silence Notifications From button.

Notifications from online applications installed on the Home Screen may be toggled on or off individually.

Time Sensitive Notifications may be activated for instantaneous notice from all applications.

How Is Your Focus Going?

Focus reduces the number of interruptions you get from friends and applications. Focus lets those who aren't on your approved list of contacts know that you can't talk right now by showing up in Messages and other applications you've authorized.

Sharing your Focus status with an app just broadcasts the fact that your alerts have been muted; the app's name remains hidden. This data is only sent while a Focus is active and if the user grants the app permission to do so.

1. In the menu, choose Focus, then Focus Status.
2. Select the Focus settings you want to share and toggle on Share Focus Status.

In a notification blackout, users should still be able to make emergency calls.

Even if your iPhone is muted or alerts are turned off, you may still receive calls and vibrations from emergency contacts.

1. Start Communicating.
2. After choosing a contact, hit the "Edit" button.
3. To activate Emergency Bypass, go to Ringtone or Text Tone and tap the button.

You might also choose a medical contact and set up a medical ID.

Schedule Or Activate A Focus

Focuses may be manually activated via the Control Center, or their activation can be pre-scheduled.

Focus on the Command Center.

1. Focus is activated by opening the Control Center, selecting it, and then activating the desired Focus (such as Do Not Disturb).

Tapping a new Focus will switch off any previously active Focuses.

The Focus settings and their duration controls are shown in the control panel.

2. Press the Do Not Disturb button, pick one choice (such as "For 1 hour" or "Until I leave this location"), and then press the button again to choose the Focus's duration and end time.

Do Not Disturb timer settings include "For 1 hour," "Until this evening," and "Until I leave this location."

Focus icons (like the Do Not Disturb button) show in the status bar and on the Lock Screen when they are activated, and your status is updated in Messages automatically. It will be clear to anybody trying to contact you that you have disabled alerts, but they may still reach out to you if it's an emergency.

You can also change a Focus on or off by navigating to Settings > Focus, touching the Focus, then turning it on.

Focus may be set to activate on a schedule.
The Focus may be set to activate at certain times, in response to specified locations, or upon launching an app of your choosing.

1. To schedule a Focus, go to the Settings menu, then hit Focus.
2. Press Smart Activation, toggle Smart Activation on and then press the Back button on the upper left to have this Focus switch on automatically depending on signals like your location or app use.
3. Select the Add Schedule button, and then decide when and where you'd want this Focus to kick in.

Your Sleep Focus will automatically adhere to your Health app-created sleep schedule. Select Open Sleep under Health to create or modify a sleeping routine. Your following night's sleep and morning alarm may be adjusted as well.

Switch Off A Focus
After utilizing a Focus, just turning it off will restore normal notification behavior. Even after a Focus has

been disabled, its entry remains in the Control Center.

1. Select the Lock Screen's Focus symbol by touching and holding it.
2. To switch focus, launch the Control Center.
3. You can switch off an active Focus by tapping it.
4. Siri-controlled on/off switching for a Focus

Siri supports the on/off functionality of a Focus.

Siri, say "Turn on the Work Focus" or "Turn off the Work Focus" to toggle the feature on or off.

Get Rid Of A Focus

You may remove a previously created Focus if you no longer need it.

1. Navigate to Preferences > Focus.
2. Select the Focus by tapping it, then swipe down to the Delete Focus option.

Focuses may be restored by navigating to Settings > Focus and selecting the Add button.

Keep Your Mind On The Road

Keep your mind on the road with iPhone concentration

If you want to keep your mind on the road, turn on the Driving Focus. When used, it reduces or disables the volume of incoming calls, texts, and other alerts. Instead of looking at your iPhone, you can have Siri read you the responses. Incoming calls are permitted only when the iPhone is linked to CarPlay—a vehicle Bluetooth® system—or a hands-free device.

Activate The Driving Focus

The Driving Focus may be programmed to activate automatically when you get into a moving vehicle. (The option to manually activate it via the Control Center is also available.)

1. To activate driving mode, go to Settings > Focus and then touch Driving.
   The Driving Focus should appear automatically; if it doesn't, choose Add in the upper right, and then select Driving.
2. To enable Focus Status sharing, choose the tab.
3. Choose who should get an automatic reply when the Driving Focus is activated by tapping the Auto-Reply button.
   - No one
   - Recent
   - Favorites

- The auto-reply you set up may be modified to suit your needs.

Then use the top left arrow to return here.

4. Select When You're Driving from the menu that appears when you tap While Driving (below Turn On Automatically).
   - Automatically, whenever your iPhone thinks you could be behind the wheel.
   - If your iPhone is synced with a car's Bluetooth system, it will work as described under "When Connected to Car Bluetooth."
   - When activated manually, namely using the Control Center interface.
   - When an iPhone is linked to CarPlay, the feature is activated automatically.

Receive texts, alerts, and calls even when traveling.
You may ignore a Driving notice if it appears when you're in a moving vehicle but you're not the driver.

Tap I'm Not Driving.

Driving Focus allows you to receive calls, texts, and alerts while in a moving vehicle.

Activate The Family Sharing Function

With Family Sharing, you and up to five immediate family members may share iCloud storage, music, apps, and other Apple services. You may also use this to assist each other in finding lost gadgets.

Everyone else in the household is invited to join in by one responsible adult. Family Sharing is instantly activated on all members' devices once they sign up. The collective then decides on the shared services and features they want to use.

Only some devices can take use of Family Sharing.

The Settings page for Family Sharing. There are five members of the family included, and four subscriptions are split among them.

Gather your loved ones together and start a sharing group!

Family Sharing requires just a single device for setup. Once you've done so, it will be accessible across any of your Apple devices.

1. To create a Family Sharing group, go to Settings > [your name] > Family Sharing and then follow the on-screen instructions.
2. Include a sibling or two. A parent or guardian may be selected when a new adult family member is added.
   It's possible to add relatives later on, too. See Insert a new iPhone user into an existing Family Sharing group.
3. Select the Family Sharing option you'd want to configure, and then stick to the on-screen prompts.

   Follow the on-screen prompts to set up Apple Cash or parental controls for a kid by tapping their name, tapping the feature, and then following the prompts.

You can check what you're sharing with your family and modify sharing settings at any moment.

Family Sharing Possibilities

You may do the following in a Family Sharing group:

- Shared passwords and passkeys allow several users to get access to a single set of resources, such as a bank account or a cloud storage service.

- Create a shared folder in iCloud Drive to store and access your family's important files and images.
- Apple and App Store memberships: iCloud+ and other Apple memberships, as well as qualified App Store memberships, may be shared.
- Content bought via the App Store, Apple Books, or Apple TV may be shared across several devices. The family planner is responsible for paying for everything.
- Sharing your location with your Family Sharing group allows everyone in the group, including new members to join at a later date, to use the Find My app to check where you are and find your misplaced device.
- Apple Card and Apple Cash: You may share your Apple Card with trusted members of your Family Sharing group or set up an Apple Cash Family account for a youngster.
- With Apple's built-in parental controls, you can keep tabs on what your kids buy and how they use their Apple products.
- A gadget for your kid: you may tailor an iPad or iPhone with parental controls to suit your family's needs.

To explore recommendations and advice regarding Family Sharing options, utilize the Family Checklist. Access the family checklist by selecting Settings > Family.

Add New Members To Existing Groups

The iPhone's Family Sharing feature allows you to add new members to existing groups.

Each member of the family needs their own Apple ID to participate in Family Sharing. Sharing subscriptions and other features in this manner is an excellent alternative to disclosing private material like images and papers.

The family organizer may quickly invite family members who have an Apple ID or establish an Apple ID for a youngster who doesn't have one yet.

The Addition Of A Family Member's Apple ID

A family member with their own Apple ID may be added by the group's organizer.

1. Select Family from the Settings menu, and then hit the + button in the top right corner to add a new family member.
2. Select Invite Others and follow the prompts.

    It's up to you whether you use AirDrop, Messages, or Mail to extend the invitation. If you're physically close to the family member, you can also hit Invite in Person and have them sign in with their Apple ID and password.

Make A Kid An Apple ID

A parent or guardian may set up an Apple ID for a kid who is too young to do it themselves and add them to the Family Sharing group.

1. To access it, go to Preferences > Family.
2. Follow any of these options:
   - If you're in charge: Create a new account for a child by clicking the "Add Member" button.
   - Remember to choose Invite Others if your kid already has an Apple ID. To accept your invitation, they may input their Apple ID password on your device.
   - Parents and guardians: Tap Add Member.
3. Follow the onscreen prompts to complete establishing the kid account. In addition to limiting access to inappropriate material, limiting screen time, and sharing your child's location with the whole Family Sharing group (including any new members joined later), you now have access to Ask to Buy. These preferences are completely flexible.

Chapter Seven

Establish Parental Restrictions

Family Sharing on the iPhone allows you to set up parental restrictions.

The organizer of a Family Sharing group has the option of enabling parental restrictions for the group's minor members. Screen Time allows parents to restrict their children's usage of iOS devices. Ask to Buy may be used to need parental permission before any in-app purchase or download can be made for a kid.

Set Up Parental Restrictions As You See Fit

The parental restrictions on a kid's device or inside Family Sharing may be set up specifically for that child. These preferences are completely flexible.

Add any of these by following the on-screen prompts during setup:

- Content in media such as applications, books, and movies may be restricted based on a user's age.
- App suspensions and use limits
- Acceptance of payments or grants of free access

Get alerts while viewing potentially offensive material.

Screen Time may scan your inbox for sexually explicit media and alert you if you or a family member have received or sent anything inappropriate.

You may restrict access to certain websites; limit what users can buy, and more.

Prepare a Kid's Screen Time Schedule Down the Road

Screen Time gives you control over sleep, app, contact, and content restrictions. Your youngster will only be able to utilize Screen Time on supported devices.

1. Select Screen Time from the menu under Settings > Family > [child's name].
2. Select the kid whose Screen Time you'd want to manage.
3. Select Screen Time and carry out the steps shown.

You may respond to your child's request for additional screen time in Messages or via Settings > Screen Time.

Ask to Buy may be activated later on for a youngster.

When a household is set up using Ask to Buy, any purchases made by children under the age of 13 need permission from a parent or guardian.

1. To access it, go to Preferences > Family.
2. Select the kid whose Ask to Buy profile you'll be creating.
3. Follow the onscreen steps after tapping Ask To Buy.

Ask to Buy has different minimum age requirements in different countries. In the United States, if a family member is under the age of 18, the family organizer may enable Ask to Buy; by default, Ask to Buy is enabled for children under the age of 13.

You may also set up an Apple Cash Family account for a kid.

Create A Child's Account
Create a child's account on an iPhone using Family Sharing.

Using Quick Start on an iPhone, the organizer, parent, or guardian may set up a new iOS device for a kid and apply parental restrictions using Family

Sharing. Without utilizing Quick Start, you can still get a kid set up with an iPhone or iPad.

Add your child's Apple ID to your Family Sharing account if they already have one. If the youngster is under 13 (the minimum age varies by location), you may establish an Apple ID for them at the time of group addition.

For those keeping score at home, you'll need iOS 16 or later. You need to activate Bluetooth.

1. Log in using your Apple ID on your iPhone.
2. On the new iPhone or iPad, you wish to set up for your kid, press and hold the side button or top button until the Apple logo shows.
3. Get your old iPhone and set it next to the new one.
4. Follow the on-screen prompts and hit Continue when your iPhone displays the Set Up New [device] screen.
   - Please choose your child's name if you are a parent.
   - To create a brand new Apple ID for a minor (someone under the age of 13), choose Create New Child Account.
5. Finish setting up your kid's smartphone by following the on-screen prompts.

Avoid Utilizing Quick Start

Avoid utilizing Quick Start when setting up an iOS device for a kid.

1. Start up the brand new gadget.
2. When the Quick Start screen opens, hit Set Up Without Another Device, follow the onscreen steps, then tap Set Up for a Child in My Family.
3. Follow the on-screen prompts to finish the installation.

All members of the Family Sharing group, including those who joined later, may access restricted material, communicate within established limitations, take breaks, share whereabouts, and use Ask to Buy. These preferences are completely flexible.

Screen Distance should be noted on compatible models.

How To Set Up Screen Time

You and your family's digital habits may be analyzed using Screen Time data, down to the specific applications and websites visited and the frequency with which devices are picked up.

Start-Up The Screen Time

Select App & Website Activity from the Settings > Screen Time menu, and then select Turn On App & Website Activity to enable this feature.

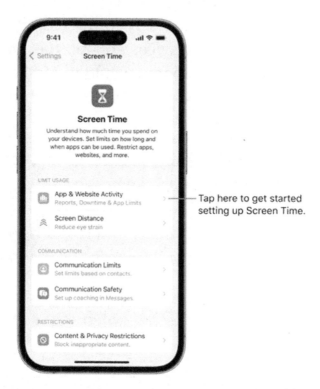

Tap here to get started setting up Screen Time.

Screenshot of the setup wizard for Apple's Screen Time app; note the option to start with App & Website Activity.

Screen Time preferences and data are synced across all of your Apple ID-signed devices.

1. Get to Screen Time in Preferences.

2. To enable sharing across devices, scroll down and toggle it on.

Read A Report Of Your Device

After activating App & Website Activity, you will be able to read a report of your device usage at any time. This report will show you things like how frequently you pick up your iPhone or other device and what applications you use the most to get alerts.

1. Get to Screen Time in Preferences.
2. First, choose the device you're interested in seeing app and website use for, then hit See All App & Website Activity.
3. Select Week to see a weekly use overview, or Day to get a daily usage breakdown.

A weekly analysis from Screen Time that breaks out app use time by user, category, and app.

Monitor Your Device Use

The Screen Time widget will allow you to quickly and easily monitor your device use.

Putting a Screen Time widget on your Home Screen is an easy way to monitor your device usage. The widget presents data from your Screen Time summary; the bigger the widget, the more data it presents.

If you've enabled Screen Time for family members via Family Sharing, you may access a list of your family members using this widget. Select a relative whose report you'd want to see by tapping their name.

When the message comes, tap the Screen Time Weekly Report to get your summary. (If the alert goes away, check the system's Notifications tab.)

Preventing Damage To Your Eyes

Screen Distance on the iPhone is a useful tool for preventing damage to your eyes.

Viewing a gadget (or a book) too closely for a prolonged amount of time may raise the risk of myopia for younger users and eye strain for users of all ages. to determine whether you've been holding your iPhone closer than 12 inches for a lengthy amount of time, the Screen Distance feature in Screen Time makes use of the TrueDepth camera (on compatible models)—the same TrueDepth camera that enables Face ID.

For younger users, Screen Distance might serve as a helpful reminder to adopt proper viewing habits that can mitigate the development of myopia. Adults may use this to lessen the negative effects of screen time on their eyes.

Screen Distance is switched on by default for children under 13 in a Family Sharing group.

1. Get to Screen Time in Preferences.
2. You may activate Screen Distance by tapping the corresponding icon.

Device Distance is an app that displays an alarm when the device is held too near to the user's face for a prolonged length of time. More than 12 inches away from your iPhone triggers the Continue button.

To safeguard your eyes, the iPhone will display a warning if you're holding it too near to your face. The caution message completely blocks the screen. When you've given yourself enough space to put your iPhone down, the Continue button will light up.

If you notice a Screen Distance warning, put more than 12 inches between your iPhone and the screen, then hit Continue.

Screen Time Configuration

Time away from screens, app use limits, and other controls may all be found under Screen Time.

Create A Break From Your Screen

Apps and alerts may be disabled for a certain amount of time so that you can disconnect from your devices. You may, for instance, plan some leisure time just before bed or before dinner.

During this period, you will have access to just the calls, texts, and apps that you have authorized. You can accept calls from contacts you've opted to allow communication with during downtime, and you may utilize applications you've chosen to allow at all times.

1. Get to Screen Time in Preferences.

2. If you haven't previously, choose App & Website Activity and toggle the switch to the on position.
3. Choose one of the following actions after tapping Downtime:
   - Enable Downtime Until Tomorrow.
   - To plan for maintenance, just use the Scheduled button.

When you request maintenance, you will get a reminder 5 minutes before the scheduled start time. You may ignore the notification, or switch on downtime until the commencement of the planned downtime.

4. Time frames may be defined for Every Day or Custom Days.

Scheduled may be toggled off at any moment to cancel Downtime.

Limit App Access And Usage
Both app categories (like Games or Social Networking) and individual applications may have their use time-restricted.

1. Get to Screen Time in Preferences.
2. Touch App Limits, then touch Add Limit.
3. Choose app categories.

If you want to restrict just certain applications, you may do so by tapping the category name, which will bring you a list of all the apps in that section. You may set a time restriction for many categories or applications at once.

4. Select a time limit by tapping Next in the upper right.

   Limits may be established for individual days by selecting Customize Days and entering the appropriate period.

5. When you're done establishing constraints, choose Add.

You may choose which contacts and applications will always be accessible.

During scheduled downtime, you may choose which applications are accessible and which contacts can be reached in the case of an emergency.

1. Open Screen Time and choose Always Allowed.
2. Tap or next to an app below Allowed Apps to add or delete it from the Allowed Apps list, respectively.
3. Select Contacts to choose who you'll share your information with.

The setting you choose in the "Communication Limits" section should be shown here. Select "Specific Contacts," and then decide from the following options:

- Pick Someone I Know: To choose which individuals will be granted access to your network.
- To add a new contact and make them available for conversation.

4. Select Back on the upper left.

Limit Your Child's Access To Certain Websites

Limit your child's access to certain apps and websites on an iPhone to ensure their safety.

You may restrict access to certain apps or websites with Screen Time's parental controls.

Restrictions On Incoming

When using iCloud, you may set up time-based or permanent restrictions on incoming and outgoing calls, FaceTime calls, and texts from certain people.

1. If you haven't previously done so, enable iCloud Contacts by going to Settings > [your name] > iCloud.
2. Get to Screen Time in Preferences.

3. Select one of the following for always-on communication (other than during downtime) by going to Communication Limits > During Screen Time.
   - For restricted access to your contacts only.
   - Lists of People and Teams Containing at Least One Contact: To restrict one-on-one chats to contacts, and to need at least one contact member to participate in group chats.
   - Everyone: To enable talks with anybody, even unknown numbers.
4. Click the Back arrow in the upper left corner, then click Offline.

   This is already set to the value you choose in Step 3 (during Screen Time). Select "Specific Contacts," and then decide from the following options:

   - Select Individuals: To choose individuals with whom to maintain touch throughout maintenance.
   - Everyone: To enable talks with anybody, even unknown numbers.

Calls and messages from people who are presently blacklisted in your Communication Limit settings will not be delivered.

The name or number of the person you are trying to contact, but are unable to due to your Communication Limit settings, will display in red in your list of recent calls or texts. When the restriction on your communications with them is raised, you may start talking to them. A Time Limit alert will appear if the restriction applies exclusively to scheduled maintenance. When the maintenance period is finished, you may contact them again.

Following the above procedures will allow you to resume communication with contacts who have been banned due to your Communication Limit settings.

Make sure no embarrassing pictures get through

In chats, AirDrop, Contact Posters, FaceTime chats, the Photos app, and third-party applications that utilize Apple's Communication Safety framework, you may have your iPhone (or a family member's iPhone) identify nudity in photographs before they are transmitted or received. Blurring the picture and providing tools to assist your youngster in coping with the circumstance if nudity is discovered (may not be accessible in all countries or areas). Using this function, Apple will not have access to your picture library.

1. Get to Screen Time in Preferences.
2. Select Communication Safety and activate it.

When the Communication Safety feature is on, an iPhone will alert the user if they try to view or send a nude photograph.

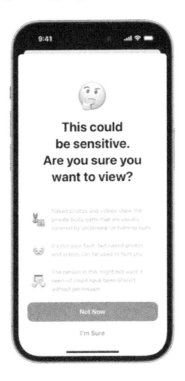

The Sensitive Content Warning screen, warning of probable nudity in a picture. The following controls are located in the screen's footer: Not Right Now, There Are Solutions, and I Have Faith.

The Sensitive Content Warning is activated in the Settings > Privacy & Security menu when

Communication Safety is on. Settings > Privacy & Security is where you'll find the option to enable the Sensitive Content Warning.

Filter Out Offensive Material

Limit Access to Private Content and Personal Information Use Screen Time to restrict access to explicit material and limit in-app purchases on iOS devices.

1. Access the Settings menu, then choose Content & Privacy Restrictions.
   You may even lock the settings with a password if you choose.
2. You may limit iTunes and App Store purchases, app use, and content ratings by selecting the appropriate choices.

You may disable SharePlay in FaceTime conversations by going to Settings > Screen Time > Content & Privacy Restrictions > Allowed Apps. To allow SharePlay, switch it on.

Configure A Family Member's Screen Time

You can monitor your family's device use with Screen Time and provide advice on how to better manage everyone's screen time. A family member's

Screen Time may be configured either on their device or, if Family Sharing has been enabled, on their device.

As the organizer of a Family Sharing group, when you set up a kid account, you may set up content limits, Communication Limits, and downtime. Parental controls may be adjusted at any time under Settings > Screen Time once the child's account has been created.

Web Content Filter and Communication Safety for less than 13-year-olds are enabled by default to prevent access to inappropriate material online.

Create A Family Screen Time Schedule

1. Access Screen Time via Settings > General on your smartphone.
2. Scroll down and choose a family member underneath Family.
3. Follow the steps outlined in Schedule time away from the screen to arrange some leisure for your loved one.

In Messages or via Settings > Screen Time, you may either grant your child's request for additional screen time or refuse it.

4. Follow the steps outlined in Set limitations for app usage to restrict your child's access to certain apps.
5. To pick applications and contacts to enable your family member to use at all times, follow the steps in pick apps and contacts to allow at all times.

   Make sure the Allowed applications list includes any necessary health or accessibility applications for your loved one. During maintenance or after the app's time restriction has passed, your loved one may not be able to send or receive messages (even to emergency numbers and contacts) if Messages aren't always permitted.

6. You may assist your family members from developing myopia and other eye problems by using Screen Distance.

Permit or forbid a family member's device to make and receive calls and texts

All or some incoming and outgoing communication with selected contacts may be disabled on your family member's device at any time. This includes phone calls, FaceTime calls, and text messages.

1. If you haven't previously turned on Contacts in iCloud on your family member's device, go to Settings > [child's name] > iCloud, then switch on Contacts.

   Only family members who use iCloud Contacts may be managed by you.

2. Select Settings > Screen Time on your loved one's smartphone.
   - Cut off contact whenever you want: Select Contacts Only, Contacts & Groups with at Least One Contact, or Everyone from the During Screen Time menu.
   - During downtime, try to limit your conversations: Use Idle Time to Tap. The option you picked for During Screen Time is already set here. You may modify this to only allow access to certain people.
     Choose from your contacts, or your child's contacts, or add a new contact if you've selected Specific Contacts for the person you wish to enable to chat during free time.
   - Using Family Sharing, you may manage your child's contacts by viewing, editing, adding, or removing people from their address book. Choose Contacts [Kid's Name> Management.

If your kid already has contacts stored in iCloud, they will get a request to manage those contacts on their iPhone. They won't be alerted if they don't have contacts, and you can start adding people right away.

To keep track of how many contacts your kid has, a new row will appear under Manage [child's name] Contacts after you begin managing their contacts. Select the row to see or change the contacts.

- To disable your child's ability to modify their contacts, tap the Allow Contact Editing button.

You may restrict your child's access to certain people and times by disabling contact editing and setting all communication to Contacts Only.

Your loved one will not be able to receive phone calls or messages from those who are presently banned by the Communication Limit settings.

A red hourglass indicator will display next to the person's name or number if they try to phone or text someone who is presently banned by the Communication Limit settings in your home. If the restriction is time-based, your loved one will get a Time Limit notification and be able to continue talking to the contact after the downtime is over

If your loved one is unable to contact certain people due to the Communication Limit settings, you may adjust these parameters as described above.

Make sure there aren't any embarrassing photos on a relative's iPhone.

Communications, AirDrop, Contact Posters, FaceTime communications, the Photos app, and third-party applications that embrace Apple's Communication Safety framework may all be set up to scan photographs for nudity before they are transmitted or received on an iPhone. Blurring the picture and providing tools to assist your youngster in coping with the circumstance if nudity is discovered (may not be accessible in all countries or areas). Using this function, Apple will not have access to your picture library.

In a Family Sharing group, Communication Safety is on automatically for any children under the age of 13.

1. Access Screen Time via Settings > General on your smartphone.

2. To contact a loved one, scroll down and click on his or her name.
3. Select Communication Safety and activate it.

   The Screen Time password may be required.

The Sensitive Content Warning is activated in Settings > Privacy & Security when Communication Safety is enabled.

Prevent a family member's access to potentially harmful online information

By adjusting the level of explicitness allowed under Content & Privacy Restrictions, you can make sure that your child's or other family member's device only contains age-appropriate material.

1. Select Settings > Screen Time on your loved one's smartphone.
2. Access the Settings menu, then choose Content & Privacy Restrictions.
3. Select custom settings for viewing and privacy.

   If you want to prevent your loved ones from experiencing hearing loss, go to the settings, press Reduce Loud Sounds and then hit Don't Allow. (This restricts the maximum volume that may be set for headphones.)

To disable SharePlay during family FaceTime chats, go to the user's device's Settings > Screen Time > Content & Privacy Restrictions > Allowed Apps. To allow SharePlay, switch it on.

4. Tap the Back button at the upper left.

It's possible to edit a family member's Screen Time settings at a later time.

You may add or modify a family member's Screen Time settings at a later time by repeating the procedures outlined above.

If you set up Screen Time for a family member on their device (not via Family Sharing), and you forget the Screen Time password, you may use your Apple ID to reset it. If you've set up Family Sharing and Screen Time for a family member on your smartphone but have forgotten the password, you may reset it using your device passcode, Touch ID, or Face ID.

Utilize iPhone Messages

You have two options for sending texts in the Messages app:

• Communicate with other iPhone, iPad, and Mac users via Wi-Fi or cellular data using iMessage.

Blue balloons represent your iMessage conversations.

- With green bubbles representing SMS/MMS messages.

Enable iMessage

1. Simply activate iMessage by going to Settings > Messages.
2. Under Settings > Messages > Send & Receive, you'll see a section labeled "You can receive messages to and reply from." Here, you can pick the phone numbers and email addresses you want to use with iMessage.

When you enable iCloud Messages on your iPhone, all of your messages, both sent and received, are backed up in the cloud. All of your chats are synced to any new device you log into with the same Apple ID, provided that device also has Messages in iCloud enabled.

1. Show All may be accessed by selecting Settings > [your name] > iCloud.
2. If you haven't previously, activate the Messages feature.
3. In the iPhone's Settings app, tap Messages > Text Message Forwarding to verify the recipients for all incoming SMS and MMS messages.

If you have Messages in iCloud enabled across your Apple devices (running iOS 11.4, iPadOS 13, and macOS 10.13.5 or later), then deleting a message or attachment from your iPhone will also erase it from all of your other Apple devices.

iCloud storage is used for iMessages.

Send And Receive SMS Or MMS Messages

If you need to send and receive SMS or MMS messages, look elsewhere.

If you haven't already, you may set up your iPhone so that any SMS messages you send or receive are synced across all of your Apple devices.

1. Choose Conversations > Preferences.
2. Select Devices to Forward Text Messages to, and then activate the desired devices.

A six-digit activation code will show on the other device if you are not using two-factor authentication.

Introduce Yourself With A Picture And Name

The Messages app allows you to introduce yourself with a picture and name. Every time you communicate with a new person, you have the option of telling them about it.

1. Launch the iPhone's Messages application.
2. Select "Edit" from the menu on the upper left.
   - Select "More" from the menu that appears.
   - After enabling Name & Photo Sharing using the Set Up Name & Photo menu, you may make any of the following modifications:
3. In your likeness: Select an option by tapping Edit underneath the circle. You may upload a custom picture, an emoji, or a Memoji.
   - Hello, Tap Name.
   - Your name and photo will be visible to: Select an option under Automatically Share and tap Done.

After setting up your profile, you may modify your name, profile image, and who can see it by selecting Edit or the More option, and then selecting Name & Photo.

When you send a message to someone using a non-Apple device, your name and picture may not show as intended.

Regarding The iPhone's iMessage

You may use the Messages app on your iPhone, iPad, Mac, or Apple Watch to send and receive messages, which are encrypted during transit.

If someone sends a message to your email address or phone number using iMessage, you get the message on all your Apple devices that are set up to receive messages sent to that email address or phone number. You can stay in contact with people no matter where you are thanks to iMessage since you can see texts received from any device.

To use iMessage, you must have an Apple ID. You have an Apple ID if you have ever made a purchase from the iTunes Store, the App Store, or iCloud, or if you have ever checked in with your Apple ID.

Messages chat displaying iMessage functionality.

What you need to know to use iMessage effectively:

- It's possible to send messages using a cellular connection or Wi-Fi.
- While iMessage conversations do not count against your monthly SMS/MMS allotment, cellular data costs may still apply.
- Messages sent and received between Apple users using iMessage look like blue bubbles. (Green bubbles represent text messages sent by SMS or MMS.)

  If the Send button is blue, your message will be sent via iMessage; if it's green, it'll be sent via SMS/MMS or your cellular connection.

- In a one-on-one chat, both participants may see whether the other is typing a response. You may also check to see whether the other person has seen your message by using seen Receipts.

  Tapbacks, message effects, collaboration, inline responses, undo send, audio messages, Memoji, garbage reporting, group chat management, and much more are just some of the applications and features that may be used.

- iMessage is encrypted before being transmitted for further safety.
- Spam and unwanted communications sent using iMessage may be reported to Apple.

Send And Receive Text Messages
Use your iPhone to send and receive text messages.

You may use the Messages app to send text messages, photos, and much more. You may respond to individual comments in a thread or remarks inside a discussion. Siri can also read and reply to your text messages.

Be sure to set up Messages so you can make use of its many capabilities.

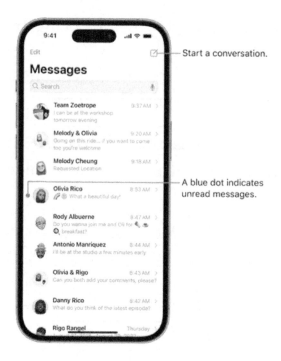

Start a conversation.

A blue dot indicates
unread messages.

There is a Compose button to the right of the discussion list in Messages. A new message will have a blue dot to the left of it until it is read.

Message Via Text

A text message may be sent to one or more recipients to kick off a discussion.

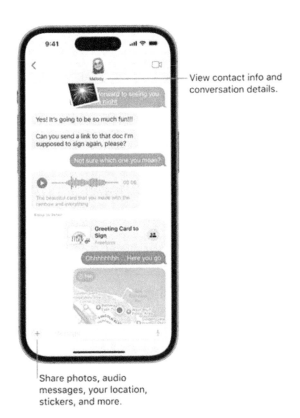

View contact info and
conversation details.

Share photos, audio
messages, your location,
stickers, and more.

A chat over Messages. At the top of the window,
you'll see the recipient's name. You may touch their
name to reveal discussion information. In the
bottom left, you'll see the plus sign.

1. Launch the iPhone's Messages application.
2. Use the top-right Compose button to start
   writing.
3. Provide each recipient's phone number, contact
   name, or Apple ID.

Or hit the Add Contact option on the right, then pick contacts from the list.

- Select the input box located above the keyboard and start typing. (Use the on-screen keyboard's Emoji or Next Keyboard buttons to insert emoji.)
- To dictate text in the keyboard's native language, use the Dictate key.
- By selecting the applications option, you can use iMessage applications to communicate your location, photographs, videos, voice messages, stickers, and more.

4. Choose the Send option to send.

If a transmission fails, a warning will be shown. To retry sending the message, just on the Send Failure button.

From inside a chat, you may access the Messages list by using the Back button.

If your iPhone is set up with Dual SIM, you may press the number as you type to immediately swap to the other outgoing line.

Get Back To Someone

In the Messages list, conversations are organized into sublists. Any discussion may be responded to. If there is a dot next to a chat, it means you have unread messages.

1. Launch the iPhone's Messages application.
2. To join a discussion, choose it from the Messages list and hit the appropriate button.
3. To send a message, press the text area, type your message, and then hit the Send button.

Get the time a message was delivered to you as a helpful hint. To see the timestamps for each message in the discussion, drag the bubble to the left.

Reply directly inside the body of a message
You may reply to a particular comment right there. An inline reply directly paraphrases the original message. This helps to keep a hectic discussion on track by making it obvious which replies go with which messages.

Everyone in the conversation can read your inline replies.

Composing an inline reply in a group chat in Messages. At the very top of the screen are miniature representations of everyone in the crew. The virtual keyboard appears in the screen's lower half. Inline replies obscure the discussion except for the precise text being responded to.

1. Launch the iPhone's Messages application.
2. To respond to a particular message bubble, swipe right on it.
3. Enter your message, and then touch the Send button.

4. To go back to the main discussion, just touch the hazy backdrop.

To respond with a Tapback sign, such as a thumbs up or a heart, just touch and hold a message.

Start a new discussion with the person you want to respond to if you're in a group chat and don't want everyone to see your message.

Tip: You may automatically let people know when you've viewed their messages. To activate Send Read Receipts go to Preferences > Messages.

Send, read, and respond to text texts with Siri

Siri can auto-reply to SMS, read them aloud, and even compose new ones on your behalf.

A phrase like Siri:

- "Tell Mayuri, tomorrow sounds good, how about it?"
- Antonio, my final communication to you, is here.
- That's fantastic news!

Siri may send a message immediately after reading it back to you. To activate this feature, go to Siri & Search > Automatically Send Messages in Settings.

Different bubbles are blue and green. Why?

If the message can be transmitted via iMessage, a blue Send arrow will show next to the Send button, and the bubble containing the message will be blue.

If the receiver doesn't have an Apple device, for example, you may still send them an SMS or MMS message. Messages transmitted via SMS/MMS are displayed in green bubbles.

A round of Messages chat amongst friends. At the very top of the screen are miniature representations of everyone in the crew. The virtual keyboard appears in the screen's lower half.

The green color of the chat boxes suggests that not everyone is using iMessage.

Receivers using non-Apple devices may not see your messages in the intended format.

Retract And Modify Recently Sent Messages
Messages allow you to unsend and modify recently sent messages, so you can go back and correct that mistake or take back the one you sent to the incorrect person by accident.

Messages' undo send and edit menus are shown. The communication is filtered so that just the chosen text is clear.

Only iMessage allows you to retract or modify sent texts.

Retract A Message

You may undo a recently sent message for up to 2 minutes after sending it.

1. Launch the iPhone's Messages application.
2. To retract a previously sent message, touch and hold the bubble.

   Both your and the recipient's chat histories will reflect the unsend confirmation.

When you click "Unsend," the recipient's device will no longer have your message.

The original message will be kept in the chat if the recipient isn't running iOS 16, iPadOS 16, macOS 13, or later. Even after you click "Unsend," the receiver may still be able to see the original message in the conversation history.

Retract a message that you've already sent

Within the first 15 minutes after sending a message, you have the option to go back and makeup to five edits.

A modified version of the previous message in a Messages exchange. The virtual keyboard takes up the bottom half of the screen, while suggestions for the currently selected word run along the top. The text message being edited stands out from the rest of the discussion, which is often lighthearted.

1. Launch the iPhone's Messages application.

225

2. Choose the thread where the message you wish to change is located.
3. Hold and hit Edit on the message bubble.
4. Just hit Send Edit to send it again with your modifications, or Cancel Edit to undo them.

   The discussion transcript indicates that the message was modified.

Both your iPhone and the recipient's device will display your changes to the message bubble, and you can both touch Edited to see prior versions of your message.

If the recipient is not running iOS 16, iPadOS 16, macOS 13, or later, all subsequent messages you send them will begin with "Edited to" and include your revised text in quote marks.

Chapter Eight

Camera For The iPhone

With A Brand-New 48MP Primary Lens

Two primary back cameras and one primary front-facing camera remain unchanged from last year's versions in both the iPhone 15 and 15 Plus. All new this year, however, is the primary camera—48 megapixels, 26 mm, f/1.6.

Reviews of the iPhone 15

Regarding the internal workings of its photo sensors, Apple is notoriously tight-lipped. Our research has led us to believe that the 48MP camera on the plain old iPhone 15 and the iPhone 15 Plus does not use the same Sony IMX803 sensor as the ones on the iPhone 15 Pro and the iPhone 14 Pro. Instead, it's a stacked Sony sensor—probably made to order—that could improve low-light performance and reading rates.

The primary camera, apart from that, is known to have 1.0μm pixels arranged in a Quad-Bayer configuration. Despite this, 24MP stills are the default thanks to Apple's computational and stacking wizardry. The main camera has PDAF and 100% focus pixels as well. On top of that, there is EIS for video recording and sensor-shift OIS for steadiness. Mounted behind the camera is an f/1.6 lens.

Reviews of the iPhone 15

The additional camera hardware is also mostly unknown to us. An f/2.4 lens encases the iPhone 15's 12MP ultrawide camera. No frills, such as autofocus, are present. That feature, exclusive to Pro models, lets the ultrawide function as a macro lens. The 12 MP f/1.9 front-facing camera, however, does have phase detection autofocus. Moreover, it is capable of improving portraiture by using depth data from the front-facing SL 3D camera.

The Features And Camera App

Since iOS 16, the viewfinder has remained essentially unchanged. Because the three cameras have been fine-tuned, you can see what's going to be beyond the frame in real time, even if you can't see it via the viewfinder.

Including last year's Photonic Engine and all heritage capabilities, Apple's picture processing includes Smart HDR, Night Mode, and Deep Fusion.

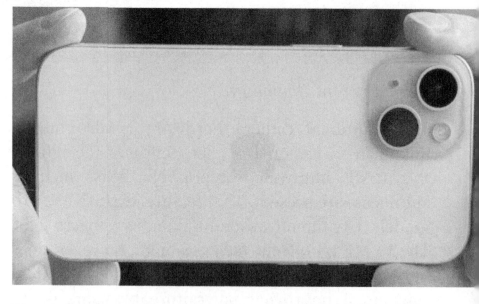

Users have no say over any upgrades other than Night Mode. When you're in a low-light situation, the Night Mode indicator will appear automatically, and you'll notice the advised seconds next to it. The

Night Mode may be disabled completely or extended for a longer period.

As usual, the cameras communicate with one another, so when you move between them, they are already set to the right exposure and tone mapping. Both video and still images are affected by this. Due to the lack of focus on the iPhone 15's selfie camera, a dedicated macro mode is not available.

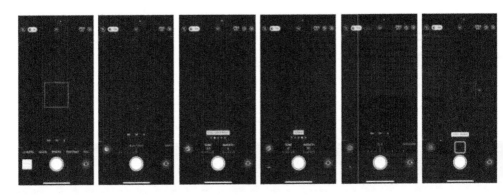

User Interface Design for the Camera App on the Apple iPhone 15 Reviews of the Apple iPhone 15's Camera App and Its User Interface

Either the primary or front-facing camera may be set to portrait mode. However, the non-Pro iPhones do not support RAW capture. Nonetheless, this year you have the option to pick between 12MP and 48MP while taking photos, rather than the new norm of 24MP from the primary camera. The first may be accomplished in the camera app's settings, while the latter can be accessed via a JPEG Max option in the camera's user interface. Below, you may see examples of the various resolution modes.

The Photographic Styles function allows for automated element-by-element editing of photos; for instance, it may make separate adjustments to the subject and backdrop. Rich Contrast, Warm, Standard, Vibrant, and Cool are your options. You may adjust the settings for each mode to your satisfaction and make the one you like most the default. It's similar to filters, except it lasts a lot longer.

Apple iPhone 15 camera settings - Apple iPhone 15 camera settings - Apple iPhone 15 review Lighting choices Review of the Apple iPhone 15 and video recording capabilities

Additionally, the cinematic mode is available, carrying over from earlier iPhone iterations. The phone captures a depth map in addition to the video, allowing you to manually modify the focus point after the fact, in addition to automated rack focus. You can use the iMovie and Clips programs to edit these kinds of films.

All iPhone 15 models retain last year's action mode functionality. For scenarios and circumstances that are full of activity and movement, there is an improved video stabilization setting.

Quality Of Daylight Photos

It should be noted right away that the cameras on the iPhone 15 are very consistent in their output, as is usual for Apple. The shot-to-shot variation is so small that we sometimes had to wonder whether we were comparing two separate files.

It should come as no surprise that the primary camera works well when the lighting is nice. Images captured with last year's 12MP iPhone 14 had noticeably less detail than the new default 24MP resolution. When compared to other Android flagships, the level of detail is even more astounding. Dynamic range and sharpness are also top-notch. An accurate comparison may be made.

Here are some examples from the 24MP primary camera of the iPhone 15: f/1.6, ISO 50, 1/5348s. This is part of our evaluation of the Apple iPhone 15. The Apple iPhone 15 review includes samples taken with the 24MP primary camera at f/1.6, ISO 50, and 1/5076s.

30MP front-facing camera samples for the iPhone 15

Color science is one of the few subjective aspects of the iPhone 15 camera that we find unappealing. Colors are mostly accurate, although we find them too subdued. However, it is nothing new for Apple cameras. The overall appearance became gritty since most shadows and the sky/clouds seemed darker than they were.

How To Capture Images Using Camera

Learn how to capture images using the Camera on your iPhone. Zoom in or out to get the perfect photo, and choose from a variety of shooting modes including "Photo," "Video," "Cinematic," "Pano," and "Portrait."

Turn On The Cam

Any of the following will launch Camera:

- On your iPhone, open the Camera app by selecting it from the Home screen.
- To unlock your iPhone, swipe left.
- Press and hold the iPhone's camera button until the Home screen appears.
- To access the camera, launch Control Center.
- Siri, tell the camera to open by saying something like "Open Camera."
- The Action button on the iPhone 15 Pro and iPhone 15 Pro Max may be programmed to launch the Camera app.

A green dot will show in the upper right-hand corner of the screen to indicate that the camera is active, which is good for your safety.

Capture a photo Open Camera, then hit the Shutter button or push either volume button to capture the photograph.

The digital camera is set to "Photo," with additional controls on the left and right of the viewfinder. At the very top of the display, you'll find shortcuts for Flash, Camera Settings, and Live Photos. The Photo and Video Viewer button is located in the bottom-left corner. Both the Take Picture and Camera Selector Reverse buttons may be found in the bottom-right area of the screen.

Modify The Camera's Settings
The default setting for the Camera is the Photo mode. Take both regular and moving pictures using

the Photo mode. The following camera modes may be selected by swiping left or right on the camera screen:

- To record a video.
- Photograph a wide vista or scene in one shot; abbreviate "pano"
- Add a depth-of-field effect to your portrait shots (on compatible models).
- Use a square aspect ratio while taking pictures.

On iPhone 11 and after, hit the Camera Controls button, then press 4:3 to pick between Square, 4:3, or 16:9 aspect ratios.

Scale In/Out

- To zoom in or out of the Camera on any device, just squeeze the screen.
- To swiftly zoom in or out, you may choose between 0.5x, 1x, 2x, 2.5x, 3x, and 5x on iPhone models with Dual and Triple camera systems. Touch and hold the zoom controls, and then move the slider right or left for a finer degree of zoom.

Prepare Your Shot Using The Camera

Prepare your shot using the iPhone's camera features.

You may utilize the Camera's editing features to get the perfect picture every time.

Focus And Exposure May Be Adjusted

The iPhone's camera automatically adjusts for focus and exposure before snapping a picture, and its face identification feature ensures that everyone in the shot is properly exposed. Do the following to make manual adjustments to the focus and exposure:

1. Open Camera.
2. Simply tapping the screen will display the region of autofocus and the current exposure.
3. The emphasis may be shifted by tapping the region of interest.
4. Adjust the exposure by dragging the slider next to the focus area.

Camera in Photo mode. The subject is brought into sharp focus in the viewfinder, and a brightness slider appears next to it.

Tapping the screen will unlock the settings once you've touched and held the focus area to lock the focus and exposure for future photographs.

On iPhone 11 and later, you may precisely adjust and lock the exposure for prospective photographs. To change the exposure, open the camera's settings by tapping the gear icon, then hit the Exposure button. Locking the exposure means it won't change until you open the Camera again. Turn on Exposure Adjustment in Settings > Camera > Preserve Settings to prevent the exposure setting from being reset every time you open the Camera.

The flash will activate automatically whenever it's required on your iPhone's camera. Before you snap a shot, do the following to manually adjust the flash:

- To activate or deactivate the automated flash, tap the Flash button.
- Select Auto, On, or Off from the Camera Controls menu, and then hit the Flash button just below the viewfinder.

Use A Picture Filter And Snap A Shot
Put some color into your shot by applying a filter.

1. Choose either the Photo or the Portrait setting in the camera's main menu.
2. Hit the Camera Controls button, then hit the Filters button.
3. Swipe left or right below the viewer to get a preview of the filters, then press a filter to apply it.
4. To capture a picture with the selected filter, tap the Shutter button.

The Photos app allows you to modify or delete any applied filters to a shot.

Start The Clock

You may set a timer on your iPhone camera to allow yourself time to get in the photo.

1. To access the camera controls, launch the camera app.
2. Tap the Timer button, then pick 3s or 10s.
3. To activate the timer, press the Shutter button.

Level Your Shot With The Help Of A Grid

To assist you in lining up your photo, you may enable the Grid and Level features in the camera's settings menu.

To better align photos and modify horizontal and vertical perspectives after taking a photo, you may utilize the editing options in the Photos app.

Use The Camera For A Self-Portrait

Make a self-portrait using the camera. Selfies may be shot in either a still image or moving picture format.

1. Turn on your iPhone's camera.
2. To use the front-facing camera, choose it from the Camera Chooser by tapping the Front-Facing button.

3. Display your iPhone.

   To expand your field of vision, try tapping the arrows within the frame.

4. To begin recording or snapping photos, use the volume controls.

Image preview in camera mode. The Photo & Video Viewer, Take Picture, and Camera Chooser Back-Facing buttons may be found to the right of the camera mode menu. You can access Flash, Camera

Settings, and Live Photos from the menu bar. They're all snapping selfies inside the frame.

To shoot a selfie that records the photo as you see it in the front-facing camera frame, rather than reverse it, go to Settings > Camera, then switch on Mirror Front Camera.

Make Movies With The Camera

The iPhone's Camera app may be used to create both regular video and QuickTake videos. Figure out how to switch shooting modes for slow-motion, time-lapse, and Cinematic effects.

Calls made over FaceTime or the phone will not record video.

Do A Video Recording

1. To use the camera for video, launch the app and go to Settings > Camera > Modes > Video.
2. To begin recording, tap the Record button or use either volume control. You're free to do the following while we record:
   - To capture a still picture, tap the white Shutter button.
   - To zoom in and out, just pinch the screen.
   - To zoom in even more (on compatible devices), press and hold the 1x icon, and then use your finger to move the slider.

3. Tap the Record button or hit either volume button to stop recording.

When the Camera is active, a green dot will show at the top of the screen for your safety.

Get High-Quality Or 4K Footage

Depending on your iPhone model, you can capture video in high-quality formats, such as HD, 4K, HD (PAL), and 4K (PAL).

1. Select Camera > Settings > Record Video.
2. To play a video on your iPhone, choose it from the list of supported file types and frame rates.

Video files are much bigger as frame rates increase and resolutions increase.

TVs that utilize the PAL video format may be found in many parts of Europe, Africa, Asia, and South America.

Switch To Active Mode

Improved video stabilization is available in Action mode on the iPhone 14 and iPhone 15 models. To activate Action mode, tap the button that says "Action Mode Off" at the top of the screen.

The iPhone is now lying flat on the table. The camera is open and in Video mode. A runner may be seen in the background of the shot. The Flash player toggle may be found in the screen's lower left corner. The Camera Settings tab may be found in the upper left corner. In the top-left corner are simple toggles to modify the video resolution and frame rate. To the upper left, the Action button has been activated. The Camera Chooser Back-Facing button, the Record button, and the Photo and Video Viewer button may all be found on the right side of the device. A runner may be seen inside the camera's viewfinder.

To reiterate, the action mode performs best in well-lit areas. To utilize Action mode when there isn't a lot of light, choose Settings > Camera > Record Video, and then toggle Action Mode Lower Light. In action mode, you can get up to 2.8K in terms of capture resolution.

Get On Camera For A Little Video

When shooting a video, "QuickTake" refers to the "Photo" setting. QuickTake videos may be recorded in the background while still photographs are taken by locking the Record button.

1. To begin shooting a QuickTake video, open the Camera app and tap and hold the Shutter button.
2. To start recording without using your hands, slide the Shutter button to the right until it locks.
   - Below the camera are two buttons labeled Record and Shutter, respectively; choose the latter to capture a still image with your video.
   - To get a closer look at your topic, just swipe up, or squeeze the screen to zoom in if you're filming hands-free.
3. To stop recording, tap the Record button.

Image preview in camera mode. In this shot, the subject occupies the bulk of the frame in the camera's viewfinder. The Shutter button, located at the bottom of the screen, slides to the right, representing the action of beginning a QuickTake movie. The video's timer may be seen in the upper right corner.

To capture a QuickTake video in Photo mode, press the volume up or down button.

QuickTake videos may be seen in the Photos app by tapping on the thumbnail.

Make A Time-Lapse Video

In Slo-mo mode, your video will record normally, and the slow-motion effect will only become apparent when you play back the video. Your video's slow-motion effects may be set to begin and end at any point you like.

1. Launch the camera and switch to slow motion.

   You can use the front-facing camera to capture slow-motion video on the iPhone 11, 12, 13, 14, and 15 by tapping the Camera Chooser Back-Facing button.

2. To begin recording, tap the Record button or use either volume control.
   While recording, you may snap a still image by tapping the Shutter button.

3. Tap the Record button or hit either volume button to stop recording.

If you press the video thumbnail and then tap Edit, you may slow down just a certain segment of the video while keeping the remainder at normal speed. Drag the vertical bars under the frame viewer to set the start and end points of the slow-motion playback.

Both the slow-motion frame rate and resolution are model-specific. Navigate to the Settings menu > Camera > Record Slo-mo to adjust the slow-motion recording options.

Toggling between different resolutions and frame rates when recording is a breeze with this helpful hint.

Make A Stop-Motion Video

Create a time-lapse film of an event that unfolds over some time, such as the setting of the sun or the flow of traffic, by taking photos at regular intervals.

1. Turn on the camera and go to the time-lapse setting.
2. Prepare your iPhone for the action you want to capture.
3. To begin recording, touch the Record button; to stop recording, touch the button again.

For better quality time-lapse recordings in low-light circumstances, use a tripod with an iPhone 12 or later model.

Create High-Quality Prores Video Recordings

Create high-quality ProRes video recordings with your iPhone.

The camera on compatible devices allows you to capture and edit movies in better quality and less compressed ProRes format.

Every camera, including the one at the front, can record in ProRes. Cinematic, Time-lapse, and Slow-mo modes do not support ProRes.

File sizes increase with ProRes video.

Activate ProRes

Apple ProRes may be enabled by going to the camera's settings and selecting "Formats" from the drop-down menu.

Start Recording In ProRes

1. To start recording in ProRes, launch the camera, go to the video mode, and then hit the ProRes Off button.
2. To begin recording, tap the Record button or use either volume control.

   You can squeeze to zoom in or out when filming with the back camera, as well as press to focus. If you want additional fine-grained control over your zoom, you may touch and hold the lens chooser and then move the dial. This works at magnification factors of 5x, 1x, 2x, 3x, and 5x, depending on your model.

3. Tap the Record button or hit either volume button to stop recording.
4. If you want to disable ProRes, just tap its corresponding button.

Up to 4K recording at 30 fps is supported in ProRes. The iPhone 15 Pro and 15 Pro Max, when linked to an external storage device, are capable of recording 4K video at 60 frames per second.

Only the iPhone 15 Pro 128 GB model supports recording in 4K at up to 60 fps when linked to an external storage device, while all other 128 GB iPhone models are limited to filming in 1080p at 30 fps.

Customize the ProRes recordings' color encoding
You may customize the ProRes recordings' color encoding in many ways.

When shooting video with the iPhone 15 Pro or 15 Pro Max, you have the option of using HDR, SDR, or Log color encoding.

1. To enable Apple ProRes, choose it from the Formats menu under Settings > Camera.
2. Choose ProRes Encoding, then choose HDR, SDR, or Log.

Look At Your Media In The Photos App

You can access all the media stored on your iPhone inside the Photos app.

How To Categorizing Images And Videos

Photos' method of categorizing images and videos

You browse Photos using the Library, For You, Albums, and Search buttons at the bottom of the screen.

Tap to navigate Photos.

Days view of the picture archive. The screen is now filled with various-sized picture previews. The time and place of the picture shoot appear in the upper left corner of the display. To choose and see more sharing and detail options for your photographs, click the Choose button in the upper right. Below the preview images, you may choose to browse the picture archive by year, month, day, or all photos. The Library, For You, Albums, and Search tabs are aligned along the footer.

- Pictures and videos may be seen in a library that can be sorted by day, month, year, or all.
- The Watch Memories feature in Photos on the iPhone allows you to see your memories alongside those you've shared and those that have been highlighted.
- Albums: Browse albums you've made or been added to, as well as your images, which have been neatly sorted into several groups, such as "People & Pets," "Places," and "Media Types."
- Enter search terms to get images that fit your criteria for date, location, caption, or content.

Select Library, then any of the following to see your media files organized by the dates they were created:

- Years: Easily navigate your picture archive by year.
- Months: Browse picture sets you made during the month, labeled after major occasions like birthday parties, family gatherings, and vacations.
- Days: View your greatest images in chronological order, organized by the time or location the photos were shot.
- Browse through every one of your pictures and videos.

If you want to zoom in or out when browsing All Photos, try pinching the screen. Photos may be filtered, zoomed in on, shown in a square format, or viewed on a map by tapping the more icon.

The finest images are highlighted in the Year, Month, and Day displays, while duplicates, screenshots, whiteboards, and receipts are hidden. To see all images and videos, choose See All Photos.

Browse Separate Images

On the iPhone, tapping a picture will expand it to fill the screen.

To see more of the image, double-tap or pinch out, then drag, then finally double-tap or pinch in to return to the previous view.

Tap the Favorite button to add the picture to your Favorites album.

To play a Live Photo while viewing it, just touch and hold the image.

Swipe to browse through your photos.

A shot with a gallery of smaller images at the screen's base. At the top left is a back button, which returns you to the view in which you were browsing. Delete, like, and share buttons along the bottom. The edit button is located at the upper right.

You may either tap the Back button on your device or drag the image down to get back to the search results.

Open Picture Or Video

Open the picture or video you want to see the metadata for, and then hit the Info button or slide up. The following specifics are visible, depending on the image or clip:

- Subjects of the photograph
- Visual-Lookup-Detected Items
- It doesn't matter whether you received the image via iCloud Shared Photo Library, Messages, or another app.
- The time and date the image was captured;
- Lens, shutter speed, file size, and other information are examples of camera metadata.
- When and where it was shot;

Tap a circle to name someone identified in the photo.

Monday · Aug 15, 2022 · 7:48 PM   Adjust
220720_DvI_Demo-Malibu_PG_J090038

Apple iPhone 14

Main Camera — 26 mm f/1.5
12 MP · 3024 × 4032 · 2.4 MB

ISO 40   26 mm   0 ev   f/1.5   1/121 s

A picture is now open in the Photos app, taking up much of the top part of the iPhone screen. Information about the picture, such as when it was taken, what iPhone model was used, what the camera settings were, and where the shot was taken, is shown in the lower part of the screen. Share, Favorite, Info, and Delete buttons are at the bottom of the screen, from left to right. The option to "Info" has been chosen.

Chapter Nine

View Photo Slideshows & Video Recordings

You may watch videos that you have recorded or stored on your iPhone by opening the Photos app. Slideshows may be made from any media in your collection, including films, images, and even Live images.

Show A Video

To watch a video on your iPhone, just touch it while you're looking at it in the Photos app. The following may be done while it is playing:

- To play, stop, unmute, favorite, share, delete, or see the video's details, touch the player controls in the bottom-right corner of the screen; tapping the screen again will conceal the player controls.
- To go between full-screen and fit-to-screen, just double-tap the screen.
- You may stop the movie by touching and holding the frame viewer at the bottom of the screen, and then you can use the left and right arrow buttons to go back and forth among the clips.

The focus of the screen is a media player. At the bottom of the screen, a frame viewer shows the video frames from left to right and an indication indicates which frame of the video is playing on the screen. Share, Favorite, Pause, Mute, and Delete buttons along the bottom of the frame viewer, from left to right.

Create A Slideshow And Show It Off

A slideshow allows you to see many media files at once, such as images and movies. Slideshows are automatically prepared and put to music.

1. Images may be seen in the Library by selecting All Photos or Days.
2. Pick by using the button.
3. To add photos to the slideshow, touch the More button after tapping each one.
4. To access Slideshow, choose it from the menu.

   While a slideshow is playing, you may touch the screen and choose Options to make adjustments to the slideshow's theme, music, and more.

Albums may also serve as the basis for a slideshow. Select Albums, then select the album you'd want to make a slideshow from.

Delete Or Conceal iPhone Media

You may erase photographs and videos from your iPhone or place them in a secret album called "Hidden" in the photographs app. Recent picture deletions are also retrievable. Hidden and Recently Deleted albums save photos you've hidden or deleted and need a passcode to see.

Using the iPhone's iCloud images feature, you may remove or hide images and have those changes reflected on all of your other iOS devices.

Erase A Picture Or Video

You may perform one of two things after tapping a picture or clip:

- Use the Delete option to permanently remove a picture from your iPhone and any other devices that are signed into the same iCloud Photos account.

  Photos and videos that have been deleted are stored in the Recently Deleted album for 30 days, during which time they may be restored or deleted permanently.

  Hide: Use the More buttons and choose Hide.

- You may find your hidden photographs in the Hidden Album. There is no other place to see them.

  If you don't want your Hidden album to show up in your Albums list, you may disable it under Settings > Photos.

  If you shake your iPhone (within 8 minutes), you may undelete or unhide the picture or video.

Hide Or Remove Multiple Media Files

You may perform one of these things while perusing images in an album, the Days view, or the All Photos view of your library:

- To erase anything, first hit Select, then tap or drag your finger around the screen to highlight its icons, and last tap the erase button.
- To conceal information, press Select, touch, or drag your finger to highlight the content you want to conceal, press the More button, and then press Hide.

Restore lost pictures or eliminate them for good

How to Recover Deleted Photos or Delete Them Permanently

1. Launch the iPhone's photo album.
2. Select Utilities from the menu, then press Recycle Bin, and last hit Recently Deleted.
3. Tap Select, then pick the photographs and videos you wish to recover or delete.
4. Select "More" from the screen's bottom, then "Recover" or "Delete."

Reveal Secret and Recently Removed Albums

Locking the Recently Deleted and Hidden albums is the norm. You unlock these albums using your iPhone authentication method—Face ID, Touch ID, or your password.

To make the secure default option the unsecure one, choose Settings > Photos > Use Passcode.

Editing Photograph On Your iPhone

Edit the photos and videos you shoot with your iPhone using the built-in tools included in the Photos app. You may play about with the exposure and color, as well as cut, rotate, and apply filters. If you decide you don't like your edits, you may undo them by tapping the Cancel button.

Any changes you make to your photographs and movies in iCloud photographs will be reflected on all of your devices.

Modify The Hue And Brightness

1. To see an image or video at its full resolution, just touch on its thumbnail under Photos.
2. You may adjust the photo's exposure, brightness, highlights, and shadows by tapping Edit and swiping left under it.
3. To fine-tune an effect, just tap it and move the slider to the desired setting.
   You can see at a glance whether effects have been scaled up or down based on the thickness of the outline surrounding the button. By tapping the

effect button, you may quickly switch between the modified effect and the unaltered one.

The Edit screen with a picture in the middle. The photo's editable controls are located below it, and the Brightness control has been chosen. You may alter the brightness using the slider located below the editing tools. The Adjust, Filters, and Crop controls may be found just under the slider. The Adjust button is chosen. The Cancel button is located in the top left corner, while the Done button is located at the top right. The Undo, Redo, Adjust,

Markup, and Plug-ins buttons are at the top of the screen as well.

4. If you're happy with your modifications, press Done; otherwise, hit Cancel and then Discard modifications.

To add filters and effects to your images and videos instantly, use the Enhance button.

Trim, Spin, Or Invert A Video Or Image

1. To see an image or video at its full resolution, just touch on its thumbnail under Photos.
2. Use the manual cropping tools by dragging the rectangle's edges to include just the part of the image you wish to preserve, or by pinching the image to choose a smaller or larger region.
   - Adjust the aspect ratio via cropping: Click the Aspect Ratio Freeform button, and then choose a desired aspect ratio from the drop-down menu that appears.
   - Use the Rotate button to rotate the picture 90 degrees.
   - The picture may be flipped horizontally with a tap of the Flip button.

Tap to undo a crop.

The Edit screen with a picture in the middle. There are three controls—"Adjust," "Filters," and "Crop"— along the screen's bottom. After clicking the Crop button, you may tweak the geometric improvements using the slider provided. The Cancel button is located in the top left corner, while the Done button is located at the top right. The Flip, Auto, Aspect Ratio, Markup, and Plug-ins buttons are also located at the top of the screen, going from left to right.

3. If you're happy with your modifications, press Done; otherwise, hit Cancel and then Discard modifications.

Pinch the image to zoom in and crop it fast while viewing it. When the image is positioned as you'd want it cropped, choose Crop from the menu in the screen's upper right. If you need to make any further changes using the crop tools, you may do so now.

Focus And Realign Your Vision

1. To see an image or video at its full resolution, just touch on its thumbnail under Photos.
2. To crop an image, go to Edit > Crop.
3. To access the available editing options, such as Straighten, Vertical, and Horizontal, swipe left beneath the image.
4. To fine-tune an effect, just tap it and move the slider to the desired setting.

By looking at the outline surrounding each button, you can see at a glance which effects have been scaled up or down according to your preferences. You may switch between the original and the modified effect with a tap of the button.

5. If you're happy with your modifications, press Done; otherwise, hit Cancel and then Discard modifications.

Use Filtering Effect

1. To see an image or video at its full resolution, just touch on its thumbnail under Photos.
2. To use a filter effect like Vivid or Dramatic, choose Edit, then select the Filters option.

   Applying Original will remove any pre-capture filters.

The Edit screen with a picture in the middle. There are three controls—"Adjust," "Filters," and "Crop"— along the screen's bottom. When you click the Filters button, a slider appears, allowing you to choose the filter's strength. The Cancel button is located in the top left corner, while the Done button is located at the top right. The Undo, Redo, Filters, Markup, and Plug-ins buttons are also located at the top of the screen, going from left to right.

3. Select a filter by tapping it, and then tweak its intensity using the slider.
   Tap the image to see how it was altered in comparison to the original.
4. If you're happy with your modifications, press Done; otherwise, hit Cancel and then Discard modifications.

Redo Several Edits

You may undo or redo several edits by tapping the corresponding buttons at the top of the screen while you work on a picture or video.

To see the difference between the original and the finalized version of a picture or video, just touch on it.

Quickly modify numerous images at once by copying and pasting changes

You may take the changes you made to one image (or video) and apply them to another, or many images at once.

1. Launch the media file that has the changes you wish to replicate.
2. Select Copy Edits by clicking the More option.
3. You may go back to your collection by using the Back button.
4. To copy and paste the changes to several images, press Select and then tap the thumbnails of the images. Or, launch a separate image or clip.
5. Tap the More Options option, then tap Paste Edits.

To produce a better match and make the photographs appear even more similar, photographs automatically change the white balance and exposure of the altered photos.

Undo The Changes To Your Picture Or Video
You can always go back to the original version of a picture or video after making edits and saving them.

1. To see more editing choices for a picture or video, open it.
2. Tap Revert to Original.

Metadata information in a picture or video may be edited

Metadata information in a picture or video may be edited to reflect a new creation date, time, or place.

1. Launch the media file in question and use the "More" button.
2. Try modifying the time and date or moving the map around.
3. After making the necessary changes, click the Adjust button.

Select, select the thumbnails you wish to edit, and then follow the instructions above to adjust the date, time, and location of many photographs at once.

Photos and videos may be reset to their original time and place of capture. Touch the More Options option, touch Adjust Date & Time or Adjust Location, and then hit Revert.

Put Your Mark On A Picture

1. Photos allow you to expand any image by tapping on it.
2. Select Edit, then select Mark Up.
3. Annotate the picture using the various drawing tools and colors. The Add Annotations option allows you to zoom in, and add a description, text, shapes, or even your signature.

4. If you're happy with your modifications, press Done to save them; otherwise, hit Cancel to discard them.

View The Forecast On Your iPhone

Check the local weather with the help of the Weather app on your phone. You can check the hourly and 10-day forecasts, learn about severe weather, and more.

The weather screen, with the current time and date at the top and the hourly forecast and 10-day prediction at the bottom. The quantity of places in the list is represented by a row of dots in the

bottom center. The Show Map and Location List buttons may be found in the bottom left and right corners, respectively.

Weather relies on Location Services to provide accurate local forecasts. Navigate to Privacy & Security > Location Services > Weather in Settings to activate Location Services. Turn on Precise Location to boost the accuracy of the forecast in your current location.

See What The Weather's Like Where You Are

When you launch the Weather app on your iPhone, the information for your current location is revealed. To add them, go to the My Location page and press the Edit Cities button.

Information on the weather, including:

- Swipe left or right to see the next hour's forecast. If you tap the hourly forecast, you'll get details like the high and low temperatures, the possibility of rain, and more for the next hour. To modify the current weather condition, tap the Chart Condition button. To see the same data for the following days, swipe right.

- See the forecast for the next 10 days, including the high and low temperatures and the possibility of rain.
- Snowstorm and flash flood alerts: View updates (not accessible in all countries or areas). If you tap the warning, you may read the official notice in its entirety.
- Check out a map depicting the current weather, air quality, or wind speeds and directions. You may tap the map to see it in its entirety, or to switch between several views, such as those that show the temperature, precipitation, air quality, and wind.
- Information on air quality may be seen, and more data on health risks and pollutant levels can be accessed (not all nations or areas provide this feature).
- When the air quality reaches a certain threshold for that place, the air quality scale will show above the hourly forecast. In certain cases, the air quality scale will always be shown on top of the hourly forecast.
- Read a news item on the local climate if one is available (may not be accessible in all countries or areas).
- More information on the weather: Check out the UV index, wind speed, visibility, moon phases,

and more as supplementary weather data. When you tap a weather detail, you'll get additional options and data about that particular aspect of the forecast.

To see how today's temperature or precipitation stacks up against typical values, touch the average weather feature.

Tap a weather detail for more information.

The weather screen, with the current location and temperature shown at the top. Information on the air quality, precipitation, UV index, and sunset time may be found in the remaining portion of the screen.

Modify The Weather Stations As Needed

For example, instead of seeing the current temperature in degrees Fahrenheit or Celsius, you may see it in miles per hour, kilometers per hour, knots, or Beauforts.

1. Launch the iPhone's weather app.
2. Select the City Edit button.
3. Select Units by clicking the More icon, and perform one of the following:
   - Select a different temperature unit by tapping either Fahrenheit, Celsius or "Use system setting."
   - Convert between several measures of speed, rainfall, pressure, and distance Select a different unit of measurement by tapping the arrows adjacent to the one currently in use.

The term "visibility distance" describes the range across which man-made features like buildings and hills may be seen.

Share The Weather Conditions

If the weather where you are is different from what is seen in the Weather app, you may send in a report.

1. Launch the iPhone's weather app.

2. Select the city you want to edit, then press More and finally Report an Issue.
3. Select the selections that most accurately reflect the current weather in your area, and then press the Submit button.

Your Apple ID is not linked to the data you provide to Apple.

Printed in Great Britain
by Amazon

43284815R00165